Biomythography Bayou

The Griot Project Book Series

Founding editor: Carmen Gillespie
Series editor: Cymone Fourshey, Bucknell University

This book series, associated with the Griot Project at Bucknell University, publishes monographs, collections of essays, poetry, and prose exploring the aesthetics, art, history, and culture of African America and the African diaspora.

The Griot is a central figure in many West African cultures. Historically, the Griot had many functions, including as a community historian, cultural critic, indigenous artist, and collective spokesperson. Borrowing from this rich tradition, *The Griot Project Book Series* defines the Griot as a metaphor for the academic and creative interdisciplinary exploration of the arts, literatures, and cultures of African America, Africa, and the African diaspora. Expansive and inclusive in its appeal and significance, works in the series will appeal to academics, artists, and lay readers and thinkers alike.

Recent titles in the series:

Biomythography Bayou
Mel Michelle Lewis

Testimony: Found Poems from the Special Court for Sierra Leone
Shanee Stepakoff

African American Arts: Activism, Aesthetics, and Futurity
Sharrell D. Luckett, ed.

*Don't Whisper Too Much and Portrait of a Young Artiste
from Bona Mbella*
Frieda Ekotto

Postracial America? An Interdisciplinary Study
Vincent Stephens and Anthony Stewart, eds.

*In Media Res: Race, Identity, and Pop Culture in
the Twenty-First Century*
James Braxton Peterson, ed.

Venus of Khala-Kanti
Angèle Kingué

Toni Morrison: Forty Years in the Clearing
Carmen Gillespie, ed.

For more information about the series, please visit
bucknelluniversitypress.org.

Biomythography Bayou

MEL MICHELLE LEWIS

BUCKNELL
UNIVERSITY PRESS

Lewisburg, Pennsylvania

Library of Congress Cataloging-in-Publication Data

Names: Lewis, Mel Michelle, author.
Title: Biomythography bayou / Mel Michelle Lewis.
Description: Lewisburg, Pennsylvania : Bucknell University Press, [2025] | Series:
The Griot Project book series | Includes bibliographical references and index.
Identifiers: LCCN 2024003589 | ISBN 9781684484812 (paperback) | ISBN
9781684484829 (hardcover) | ISBN 9781684484836 (epub) | ISBN 9781684484843 (pdf)
Subjects: LCSH: Lewis, Mel Michelle. | African Americans—Alabama—La Batre,
Bayou—Biography. | Gender-nonconforming people—Alabama—La Batre,
Bayou—Biography. | La Batre, Bayou (Ala.)—Biography. | African Americans—
Maryland—Baltimore—Biography. | Gender-nonconforming people—Maryland—
Baltimore—Biography. | Baltimore (Md.)—Biography. | LCGFT: Creative
nonfiction. | Autobiographies. | Essays.
Classification: LCC F334.B36 L48 2025 | DDC 976.1/22092 [B]—dc23/eng/20240410
LC record available at https://lccn.loc.gov/2024003589

A British Cataloging-in-Publication record for this book is available
from the British Library.

References to internet websites (URLs) were accurate at the time of writing. Neither
the author nor Bucknell University Press is responsible for URLs that may have
expired or changed since the manuscript was prepared.

♾ The paper used in this publication meets the requirements of the American
National Standard for Information Sciences—Permanence of Paper for Printed
Library Materials, ANSI Z39.48-1992.

bucknelluniversitypress.org

Distributed worldwide by Rutgers University Press

Contents

Part 3: Earth

Part 4: Mineral

Part 5: Nature

Acknowledgments

I write with deep gratitude, honoring the Ancestors, their
stories, and knowledges that inspired this book.
I have asked permission to speak.
I write with deep gratitude, honoring my family, my parents,
and all the kinfolk, the bayou of my being.
I write with deep gratitude, honoring my wife, Kerrie Cotten
Williams; your love, inspiration, support, partnership, and our
laughter are on each page.
I write with deep gratitude, honoring the work of my writer,
teacher, artist, mentor-friend, and chosen family, Adela C.
Licona, who was the guardian of each word.
I write with deep gratitude, honoring the work of poet,
multidisciplinary artist, and kindred, Ailish Hopper,
for sifting these grains of sand.
I write with deep gratitude, honoring my beloved community
who sustained me in and through these tellings: Wendy
Gaudin, Gina Breedlove, Seble Dawit, Nana Osei-Kofi,
Angelo Robinson, Kelly Brown Douglas, La Jerne Terry
Cornish, Sheri Parks, Leslie Lewis, Marjorie Pryse, Iyun
Ashani Harrison, and Iquail Shaheed. I give thanks for the
touch of healers, gift of artists, the depth of writers, and
alchemy of music makers on this journey.

Land and Labor Acknowledgment

I acknowledge the Traditional Custodians of the land on which I work and live. I recognize a continuing connection to land, water, and community.

I acknowledge that *Biomythography Bayou* was composed on the ancestral lands of the Piscataway and Susquehannock peoples, who have been joined through the northern migration by Lumbee and Cherokee communities in this region we now call Baltimore.

I honor all traditional custodians of this region.

I pay respect to the Afrodescendants who tilled and labored on this land, who were bought, sold, and self-emancipated on this land. I recognize a continuing struggle for liberation in the Baltimore region's Black communities.

I acknowledge the intentional congruence of settler colonialism and enslavement as well as intentional acts of restoration through resistance and relationship.

Passive acknowledgment is not enough to restore stolen lands and stolen people. May this statement be a part of the work to build reciprocity, solidarity, and restoration.

I pay respect to Elders and Ancestors.

Biomythography Bayou

Molasses Ballet. Digital photograph by Mel Michelle Lewis, 2023.

Conjure Portal

Last night I dreamed my family was gathered for a reunion,
down to the house.
The bayou flowed slowly.
The ocean lapped.
The moss in the great oak trees swayed.
The tastes from the kitchen wafted.
The laughter of the children swelled.
The Grandmothers' instructions echoed.
The Uncles' banter blossomed.
Everything gentle and deliberate, the pace of noticed dreams.

I entered the "family room" where my mother was attempting to nail a croaker to the wall by the fins. I begged for its life, and she gave it to me to put back in the ocean. I held the slippery scaly croaker by the tail and ran out the front door, both gasping.
My little child legs were chubby and sluggish, the pace of noticed dreams.
The croaker wriggled and sang his death song, a deep lament. Halfway between the front door and the ocean, I laid him down on the oyster shell path to rest. This did not improve his condition. His ocean insides began to spill out.
I begged him not to spill it all, yet. I promised he would soon be back in the water. I flung him out past the seawall and into the gulf. I noticed then that all of the fish, large and small, were split, segmented.

Spilling out.
But they all kept on swimming. My croaker kept on swimming.

Reasons

I haven't been *down to the house* since Mardi Gras, four years past.
The first reason is complex and painful.
The second reason is complex and painful.
The first reason is wedding related.
The second reason is pandemic related.
My family's land is unsinkable, between Mobile Bay and Grand
    Bay.
White columns
A garden
Old oaks
Slow bayou
Gulf waves
Flat Acres
Family ways

Mobile, Alabama hosted the first Mardi Gras in North America, in 1703. In my cultural and familial context, most things are Mardi Gras related, wedding related, or Mardi Gras–wedding related. Almost everyone I have ever known in life, relatives and community, has gotten married or had a party *down to the house.* My wife, librarian and archivist Kerrie Cotten Williams, and I both have roots in Black Mobile. We wanted to have our own queer Mardi Gras marriage celebration, *down to the house.* We went, to be invited.

Thirty minutes before the Mystics of Time parade
In Wintzell's Oyster House on Dauphin Street
In a building built by my wife's family
Frequented by generations of my family

For celebrations
We asked
To be invited

The first reason a queer Mardi Gras marriage celebration did not happen was an invitation to do so was not extended to us. Pelican wings folded. Fishing line cut.

Lightning
Strike
Oak

Smoke
Cold
Stun

The Ancestors were with us. Kissing our foreheads, patting our hands, smoothing our hair, cupping our chins. The sound of smiling with no teeth and jangling coins in work jumper pockets was there. The soothing of "ise'gon be alright" and "hesh now chile" was there. The smell of powder and the taste of medicine were there. We paid our fried seafood bills with deep breaths and dollars, we rose from the family-set table and made our way around the corner to Dauphin Street for the parade, together.

Months later, we invited my parents to join us at my wife's family reunion in New Orleans. Kin gathered, laughter and music punctuated our connectedness.

Hair salon
Dry cleaner
Class mate
Piano teacher
Lunch carryout
Burial Ground

We enjoyed our families and their interwoven histories.

As we said our goodbyes in a quiet corner of the French Quarter Marriott, tall windowpane overlooking the bend in the Mississippi River, my parents invited us to have a "private" dinner *down to the house*. We declined that offering, a stale alternative to the many large festive weddings held every year.

Invited
To bake
A fallen
Cake

The reason a queer Mardi Gras marriage celebration did not happen was a failed compromise. Offered with love, an unendurable concession.

The Ancestors hummed low, "Steal away, steal away home."

On a sunny warm Friday, we proceeded to the justice of the peace in Baltimore where we reside, then had a fabulous series of summer parties and celebrations with friends and affirming family. On the weekend before Mardi Gras, we hosted a huge spring party and parade in front of our Baltimore rowhome. I felt I may never choose to return to Alabama, or at least, I would never go back *down to the house*. In fact, I swore I wouldn't in texts to my parents, and in my heart.

I broke a moss-covered oak stick from the yard and placed it on my altar.

I felt shunned, after the pain of coming out in my teenage years, and then so many years of building relationships back, after relational hurricanes, over and over. After learning to feel at home again and marrying a woman who shares much of my history and community, it felt unthinkable, to go back.

However, this dynamic of rejection changed with the COVID-19 pandemic.

Now, I could not go.

The second reason a queer Mardi Gras marriage celebration did not happen was the pandemic. Family members became ill, some passed away. Hurricane season, then the next, were particularly devastating; elder family members displaced and distressed, and I could not travel. I could not help.

Still
I cannot go
I have not gone
Down to the house

Ritual

Biomythography Bayou is a balm.

Much of this book was written in quarantine, in the COVID-19-delineated isolation, drawing upon my well of memories and dreams. I had never wanted to go home as an adult, felt homesick, had never wanted to be there beyond obligation, until now.
Place your hand gently on your heart. Think of home. Deep breath.
We are still in a pandemic; even with vaccines and political changes, I do not know when I will be back there. For now . . .
Biomythography Bayou is a portal.

Griots

Last night the Ancestors gathered at the foot of the bed. For those of us who are Griots, seers, elders, and healers, we know this visitation is and is not a dream.

The Ancestors often come to see 'bout me, assist me, warn me, teach me, scold me, laugh with me, write with me, and share their wisdom.

Sometimes they keep me up. Last night they gathered to soothe me and my night questions, and give me rest.

Some in soft delicate billowing fabrics
Others in heavy organic weighty textiles
Some are peoplespirit
Others are spiritpeople
The Griot with the Hands
Held a small colorful earthen bowl
Many of them did
The Griot with the Hands

Lifted the quilt, uncovering my feet, and set my heels parallel, flexing my feet back, showing my soul to the gathering. They conferred; I lay still, not asleep, not awake. The middle way of being.

They quietly decided
They decided quietly
The Griot with the Hands
Used a fingertip to stir the contents of the bowl
The others with bowls did this
The Griot with the Hands
Bent down to hold my foot firmly, and wrote on it using the
    contents of the bowl
Many of them did

The path I walk is written on my soul

Soul Writing

I'm not sure if I have ever been an "academic." I have a BA, MS, MA, and PhD in women's studies (yes, really). I got a tenure track job right out of graduate school, I earned tenure, and was a chair and director of departments, centers, and academic divisions, administrating interdisciplinary fields of study and engaging intersectional praxis. I've published journal articles and book chapters, many of which I hardly recall. I've left "the academy" to embark on a new journey as a nonprofit executive, working at the intersection of social and environmental justice. I am also now enrolled in an environmental policy MPP program (yes, really), and spend my days working to protect wild rivers, restore damaged rivers, and conserve clean water for people and nature.

I am writing from my soul. I have been trained to write "authoritatively" in ways that I am unlearning on the page. In this voice, I am not a representative of or authority on the cultures or communities or histories or diasporas or families I design and detail in this biomythography, but I write with intention, care, and connectedness. I am accountable to my interpretations and ask for grace as I take up soul stories.

Choreography

Growing up, I was very serious about ballet (yes, really). I attended magnet performing arts junior high and high schools and was a "junior" member of a professional ballet company. I went to college on a dance scholarship and believed I would be a professional dancer and choreographer. My freshman courses in women's studies, sociology, and, later, Africana studies changed that trajectory, although I continued to dance, take creative writing classes, make visual art, and win poetry awards during my undergraduate years.

As a senior, I encountered scholarship by and about Black queer people for the first time, in a womanist theology course taught by Dr. Kelly Brown Douglas. Not personally or intellectually having (knowingly) encountered any other out Black folks who were queer, I thought I must be the only one in the world. (Although there were rumors about one Black singer, Tracy Chapman, who the young white lesbian feminists in my dorm liked; she used a lot of "you" pronouns in her songs, which I learned was a mysterious folk singer secret code.)

It hadn't occurred to me that:

> There were Black queer authors, theorists, and artists.
> I could research on these folks.
> I could be smart enough to "do" Black queer feminist scholarship myself.
> I could be a Black queer author, theorist, and artist.

This might seem naive, or even implausible, but it was the dance I was dancing. I did not have Black queer and affirming elders, until I did.

I immediately abandoned my creative pursuits in ballet and poetry. I shaved my head. With my emerging feminist analysis, flourishing queer identity, and burgeoning "Black and proud" self-concept, I began to feel dance and creative writing were deeply problematic, fraught with racial and gender inequities. Instead, I moved on to a pas de deux between graduate school and the Black gay clubs of Washington, D.C., and Baltimore.

Although I was excited to explore Black queer feminism in graduate school, my research and writing for my degrees, then for tenure and promotion to associate professor, then with an eye toward full professor, were all missing something. These degrees, and tenure, the process of earning them, my Black queer feminist faculty "possession" of them, did not have soul. The Ancestors had something to say about that. I gave up the tenure I'd worked so hard to "earn" and the trajectory I was convinced would fulfill my personal and professional dreams.

I was not dreaming.

Certainly, I acknowledge my viewpoint reflects many privileges. I know how many lives were spent living for me to have these opportunities. I am soul writing, so I must tell all of the truth. I invite you into *Biomythography Bayou*.

Decolonial Writing

Although "narrative portraiture" can refer to research practices such as oral history, painting, or photography practices, I adapt this term for this manuscript, which features a decolonial viewpoint, a "rescript" that makes available multigenerational blood memory, nonlinear time, and spiritual connection. Eurocentric epistemologies are drowned down deep. Each section of the text opens with an explicatory essay, animating the powers of particular elements in nature and thereby offering context to history, location, community, and cultural specificity. These essays bring together autobiography and mythography with Black queer feminist scholarship. They're followed by a collection of thematic narrative portraits which maintain a relationship with the element and with one another; they embody nonlinear generational connection, scene, setting, and theme.

Biomythography Bayou is a narrative portraiture project featuring experimental performative soul writing. My shift has opened me up as a "maker." I am experimenting, yet my writing is rooted in the anthropological narratives and cultural analyses, both fiction and nonfiction, of Zora Neale Hurston and the political poetic portraits of Gwendolyn Brooks. As a scholar, my poetry and prose also require a particular Black feminist citational practice. Influenced by Audre Lorde's biomythographic form, Alexis DeVeaux's articulated embodiments and queering of time, and Octavia Butler's historical harkening and speculative futurist meditations, *Biomythography Bayou* quilts contours of Black queerness and kinship across place and time, from enslavement in the deep south to liberatory loving in the digital world. I situate my work among Black and queer essayists and scholars who are also creative writers. My style is influenced by the queer narrative architecture and social critiques of Leslie Feinberg and Dorothy Allison. My magic is fortified by the poetic voices of Nikky Finney, Luisah Teish, and Susan Griffin. My beloved colleagues and Black feminist sister friends, Alexis Pauline Gumbs and Bettina Judd, and Black feminist pleasure activist adrienne maree brown illuminate my way forward, into healing feminist Afrofutures.

With an emphasis on queer, intersex, trans, and femme embodied knowledges, I engage West African worldviews, Poarch Band of Creek Indians histories, and Black Catholic Creole cosmology, offering readers archival histories, contemporary political discourse, and tellings from my ancestral imaginary. I use these as frames for the structure of the manuscript which is inspired by Dagara culture as revealed through the work of Patrice Malidoma Somé. He transitioned soon after I completed my first round of revisions for this book; I am grateful for his work and seeing. Creek wisdom and Black Catholic Creole cosmology show up in narratives as I explore family and community. Narrative portraiture appears in many forms throughout this text, including folktales, recipes, praise songs, spells, and invocations.

Borrowing inspiration from the organization of chef Mashama Bailey's The Grey restaurant menu and the elemental structure of the Dagara cosmological wheel, *Biomythography Bayou* is organized into five sections: Fire, Water, Earth, Mineral, and Nature. Bailey's menu is a journey through "dirt, water, pasture, pantry," each course offering delicious specificity yet revealing elemental relationships. *Biomythography Bayou*'s structure echoes this prix fixe menu with individual yet interrelated narratives of people and place. Somé describes fire as the mediator between the spirit world and this one, water brings cleansing, reconciliation, purification, and peacemaking, earth is the mother who is inviting us to come home, mineral speaks to our bones and invites us to remember, and nature asks us to open to transformation in order to realize our purpose.[1] *Biomythography Bayou* engages these elemental characteristics as a soul writing ritual.

Ritual Writing

I was rooted and raised in the Gulf South; my writing explores queer of color nature writing themes in rural coastal settings and southern port cities; specifically, the communities in and around Mobile, New Orleans, and Biloxi. *Biomythography Bayou* presents these ancestral lands, lineages, and queer longings as experienced in local and regional Black southern folklore, dialect, foodways, religious and spiritual practices, music, and cultural events. These are celebrated in the portraits and conveyed from the first-person viewpoint of the narrative characters whose generational and place-based connections reveal themselves throughout the text. I use the term biomythography to describe this aspect of the book. In "'The Whole Story Is What I'm After': Womanist Revolutions and Liberation Feminist Revelations through Biomythography and Emancipatory Historiography," Stacey Floyd-Thomas and Laura Gillman write:

> Biomythography, a term first coined by Audre Lorde in her personal testimony, *Zami*, can be defined as a "deliberate amalgamation of autobiographical fact and mythically resonant fiction" that locates the struggle for moral agency and self-identity in a context of social oppression.[2]

In keeping with Mississippian worldviews and Muscogee Creek belief systems regarding the cycle of birth and death, *Biomythography Bayou* has multiple narrators. As the author, I speak through each of them.

> Ancestors are mythical and material
> I feel them watching on the wall
> I hear them in waking dreams
> I visit them on the land
> I summon them on altars
> I translate them onto the page

The sound of the Black south resonates through apostrophes, abbreviated spellings, and intentionally inconsistent vernacular, chaotic and heard. Generational connections raise the possibility

Map of Mobile Bay, 1950. Reproduced with permission by the Alabama Department of Archives and History.

of these narrators embodying the same spirit across time and place, and through my voice. Andres C. Walker and David E. Balk assert:

> The essential Creek reality is a genderless, universal energy. . . . At the end of winter, spring returns, and after a full moon a new moon begins. This perspective of life and energy in the world promotes a circular notion of life and death. The meaning Creeks associate with death involves transition and impermanence, and some rituals reflect this perspective.[3]

Biomythography Bayou is a ritual.

Portal Invocation for the Reader

This text is written on the page but invites you to embody, too:

Listen
Taste
See
Smell
Touch
Feel
Be
Welcome

Audio recordings are available at melmichellelewis.com/audio.

PART 1

Water

Lemon Water. Digital photograph by Mel Michelle Lewis, 2023.

Elemental Essay: Water

Water speaks through me. What does water know?

Confluence ~ Flowing Together
Gulped down by the marshlands along the coast at the
confluence of Chickasaw Creek and Mobile River,
Plateau Cemetery is my ancestral home.
The Descendants
Live
The Ancestors
Lie
The Waters
Lap
The Bay

Barracoon: The Story of the Last Black Cargo[1] is the story of Kossula
"Cudjo" Lewis and his community in Plateau, Alabama, in 1927.
Author, anthropologist, and filmmaker Zora Neale Hurston
shares Kossula's firsthand account as a survivor of the *Clotilda*
and the community of formerly enslaved Africans said to have
been the cargo of this "last slave ship." My people lie all'round
Kossula's commemorative gravestone marker in Plateau Ceme-
tery. Folks in my family say no one knows exactly where in the
graveyard his body is buried, so they placed the headstone near
the entrance, on high ground. Most of the graves lay low and

wet. Their thirst for life quenched. Hurston writes of Kossula's thirst:

> I waited but not a sound. Presently he turned to the man sitting inside the house and said, "Go fetchee me some cool water." The man took the pail and went down the path between the rows of pole-beans to the well in the daughter-in-law's yard. He returned and Kossula gulped down a healthy cup-full from a home-made tin cup.[2]

I tip-toe through the wet mud, gulped full of folk. I place
    flowers for my Ancestors.
Most folks who know a little bout it
Know Cudjo Lewis
Most folks who know a little bout it
Know Plateau as "Africatown"

At the premiere in the community of the Netflix documentary *Descendant*, my family was in attendance. The film, like this book, is a path to the well mentioned above in Hurston's retelling of her afternoon with Kossula, a drink from his home-made tin cup.

Plateau sits just north of Magazine Point and the opening of Mobile Bay. Both sides of my family flow through this and adjoining communities. Folks in my family call it Plateau rather than Africatown. No one in their generation called anything they loved "African," it was taboo at best, and could be used as an insult to elicit shame. Folks in my family say folks from Plateau who know the river have known where the *Clotilda* (we say Clo'teal) wreck is for generations, it was just too dangerous and painful for stolen people to say so in mixed company.

White folks love to "discover" drowned known.

My last name, my father's family name, is Lewis. Folks in my family say Cudjo Lewis ain't the *exact* same Lewis as we are. Folks say we were called Lewis before he arrived. Folks on my maternal and paternal line lived in or moved through Plateau, working timber and in mills on the river. Folks on my paternal side came down from farms up the river a ways, through Plateau, into the urban Black communities of Mobile.

Rented house help
Old oak low
Come stay here
Go work hard

As an anthropologist, Hurston inquired about Kossula's legal name, Lewis. Kossula said, "[O-lo-loo-ay, my father's name] too long for de people to call it. It too crooked lak Kossula. So, dey call me Cudjo Lewis."[3] As Hurston reports, "O-lo-loo-ay" became "Lewis" for Kossula. Lewis was a community name, to be drawn up as a sound, and as kin, like Chickasaw Creek flowing alongside the Mobile River. I claim Kossula as my kin, the cemetery and our names, water in our tin cups, as the confluence. Cudjo knew Lewises—he became one.

My mother was born in Plateau. Many plots of family land and streets with family names remain. Adams, another name of *Clotilda* descendants, but who are they, and are they related to us? Murky water. Many of my relatives still live in Plateau and Prichard. The census indicates my mother's great-grandfather was a ship stevedore, unloading cargo on the docks. We may never know how close the confluence of Hurston's documentation of *Barracoon* might be to our family, but the factual documentation of our connections to the Meaher family, the *Clotilda* family, is quite compelling.

River Witness

The 1850 Slave Schedule for Mobile County lists "Adams" with fifteen dashes, representing fifteen enslaved persons, their sex and ages indicated. The very next name on the page is "Maher" listing another fifteen enslaved persons. The 1880 Federal Census lists my mother's paternal great-grandfather Nelson Adams as a "stevedore," living next door to the Meaher (spelled with an *e*) family who owned the *Clotilda*, working (for them, presumably) on the docks. This was twenty years after the schooner brought captives from the port city of Ouidah in Benin, initiated by Timothy Meaher. William Foster, captain of the *Clotilda*, listed as a shipbuilder, is documented as living just down the road. The 1880 Federal Census also notes my mother's maternal great-grandfather "works in sawmill," living a few houses away from Cudjo and his family; Cudjo is listed as "making shingles."

The 1910 Federal Census lists my maternal great-grandfather as a boomsman, rafting timber on the river. The 1910 Federal Census also lists Cudjo, age seventy-eight, and my maternal grandfather, age two, on the same page, living a few houses apart on Magazine Point Road. The 1920 Federal Census lists Cudjo, age eighty, and my maternal grandmother, age eight, with her adoptive mother and father, listed as a "lumber mill driver," living a few houses apart on Magazine Point Road.

> Yes, the Federal Census was every ten years.
> Yes, Cudjo's age in his own measured time was as he said, aged two years in ten.
> Yes, my maternal grandmother's age was estimated in all government records; she was adopted.
> Yes, her adoptive parents knew her birth parents.
> Yes, my maternal grandmother knew her birth parents.
> Yes, my mother knows her mother's birth families.
> Yes, my mother and her siblings submitted an affidavit in order for my grandmother to receive a birth certificate in the 1980s. It said she was born in 1911. They gave her one, after her children swore under oath that she existed. She did.
> Yes, erybody know bout that.

In the preface to *Barracoon*, Hurston writes:

> This is the life story of Cudjo Lewis, as told by himself. It makes no attempt to be a scientific document, but on the whole he is

rather accurate. If he is a little hazy as to detail after sixty-seven years, he is certainly to be pardoned.[4]

Pardon me. The methodology of this writing is soul science, hazy, but on the whole rather accurate.

Folks in my family are curious about who flows in their veins, have sent out tin cups of DNA to measure what's in the pail. Benin, Kossula's homeland, appears with various percentages; I am poured with 10 percent Benin and Togo, among my ancestral streams. Folks in my family are saltwater and freshwater. Brackish.

Headwaters

Growing up, I visited the many generations of my extended family, living along the western banks of the Mobile-Tenesaw River Delta, in Plateau, Prichard, and Toulminville, near the Toulmins Spring Branch of Three Mile Creek. My immediate family's home where I was rooted and raised is a few hundred feet from the Gulf of Mexico, fortified among Portersville Bay, Fowl River, Bayou La Batre, Bayou Coden, and Bayou Como. My family is rooted on the land/water of Mon Louis Island, Fowl River, and Dauphin Island. These are my headwaters.

The Source

I've lived in many homes, in many states, and even out of the country; I've lived away from coastal Alabama for longer than I lived there. But gulf-lapping land is my font. As a Black queer feminist now doing equity work in the environmental justice sector, I return to these headwaters infrequently.

Beware of the Undertow

As a teenager, I swam against the tide, gasping for air, mind, body, and spirit exhausted by coming out as queer, while also grappling with dissonant racial, religious, and class cognizance. I was thirsty for knowledge; I needed to emerge from the murky ideas surrounding me; racism, Catholicism, conservatism, militarism. I was consumed by a deep and significant thirst for justice and liberation.

I Diverted

My waters are now the Chesapeake Bay, at the confluence of Harriet Tubman and Frederick Douglass. Baltimore's harbor has rescued me many times over. I've had the will to leave at times, briefly, only to return to this urban wellspring for water. In *Pedagogies of Crossing: Meditations on Feminism, Sexual Politics, Memory, and the Sacred*, M. Jacqui Alexander writes, "Only water can rescue the intent of the will—only water and love."[5] Baltimore city loves me back; Maryland is home. However, there is still the water and love of the Gulf South, even with the undertow and shoals to navigate. Writing the creative works in this section are water/love/rescue.

Shoals ~ Writing Refractions

The shoals show themselves as the tide recedes. Collecting sediment, arising from the seabed, they pose a danger to navigation. As I write, I begin to hear the rushing, a question, "How do we tell the 'truth' in fiction?" In *The Black Shoals: Offshore Formations of Black and Native Studies*, Tiffany Lethabo King writes, "The shoal is a place, a site of disruption, a slowing of momentum, and a process of rearrangement [that] takes on various forms."[6] In this section, with water as its elemental theme, I write in various forms: poems, essays, praise songs, and recipes. All stories rearranged by water. As I write, I am moored on the shoals of hesitation. Shoals can be dangerous for navigating large vessels through short stories, but shoals can also protect sensitive estuaries where young memories live. They build up their deposits over time, barrier islands that protect and heal.

Fish also school together, forming shoals. I write in silver refractions and reflections of truth, looking down upon shoals of fish under the water from a boat. The Ancestors gather, swimming together adorned in shimmer, their stories bubbling up in refractions.

Memory is a shoal.

Water and the Word

The confluence of memory and fantasy in this section offers my reflections on water, place, and queer longings. The first selection, "Catfish Mardi Gras Queen," is a celebratory expression of a new queer folktale. This narrative portrait offers the possibility of personified hurricanes and queer rereadings of Mardi Gras preparation and festive cultural practice. The second narrative portrait representing the element water, "Bayou Honeyman," is told in the trickster tradition, at the confluence of West African and American Indigenous tales of shape-shifting and charm. This tale highlights the Mobile Bay watershed as place, and explores intersex joy and embodied pleasure, through the lens of queer sexualities, desire, love, and family. This watershed flows with honey, down into a sensual corporeal basin.

Revered chef and cookbook author Edna Lewis, who influences my writing, cooking, and dreaming, writes, "Over the years since I left home and lived in different cities, I have kept thinking about the people I grew up with and about our way of life,"[7] in her book of recipes and reminiscing, *The Taste of Country Cooking*. Her sensory memories are shared in stories and recipes. "Water Recipe," the third work in this section, explores narrative portraiture in recipe form, as homage. Recipes are instructions, histories, nourishings, and connections. Recipes are potions and spells: for birth, for death, for love, and for leaving well enough alone. Recipes are for shape-shifting. Recipes invite us to the table and send us on our way.

"A Praise Song for Blue Crab" is the final entry for this section. I honor Salif Keïta as a musician and Griot in the Malian tradition. Through "Praise Song for Blue Crab," I explore the capture of the

Blue Crab as a metaphor for the transatlantic slave trade, centering the confluence of entrapment and emancipation. Keïta is known for his "soaring, melismatic vocals and often deeply traditional lyrics, expressing the values of Mande culture" and a "traditional [but] syncretic" style.[8] I also cite the influence of Kim TallBear: "Symbiogenesis tickles me. It sounds to me like 'we are all related.'"[9] I adopt these features in form and tradition, applying them with reverence to one of my favorite Gulf South beings, the Blue Crab.

Water Invocation for the Reader

May you dip into the water
Allow it to lap against your skin
May you breathe the salt air
Feel the heaviness in your chest
May you splash
Awash with delight

Catfish Mardi Gras Queen*

You just like yo daddy
Dis said and meant all kindaways

I. RELATIONS
Dey call me Jr.
Even tho I got a brother
He go by Dubois
He call me Jr. too

Dubois a blue heron
He regal and ready
For Mardi Gras
He slick his hair and shine his shoes
He slow and pretty
He go out clean and come back clean
He still and sharp
He like to see and be seen
He like to look but don't touch
Dubois don't like no trouble

I's a steady oak tree
I's brown and green and taut

* Originally published in *Auburn Avenue*, Autumn/Winter 2019.

I's fixed and fine
I come and go with ghosts
I's magic familiar
I's Spanish moss in the breeze
I ain't no lady

Ladies talk
Dey jus say I'm trouble
Dey jus say, girl you betta come gimme some sugar
Dey jus say, umph
You just like yo daddy

II. LADYFRIENDS
Taint nuthin wrong wit ladyfriends
Folks round here known Ms. Isidore and Ma Chevery all
    they life
Red got a ladyfriend in town now too
Taint nobody down dis way seent whoitis yet
Cept Dubois and he ain't said nuthin
He let Red drive his Cadillac
He let Red wear his sport coats
She careful and fill up the tank
She shine the rims and the windows
She dry-clean his jackets
They both good at being friends and keepin confidence
Dubois don't like no trouble

Taint nuthin wrong wit ladyfriends
Ma Chevery can fix on your boat for a Sunday dinner plate
Clean your catch for a jar of fresh lemonade
Repair a cast net for a pecan pie
She jus like her daddy
Captain Chevery
Erybody know bout dat

Ma Chevery's ladyfriend es Ms. Isidore
Sew gowns and drink wine
Sing French and drink wine
Garden flowers and drink wine
Pray rosary and drink wine
Do hair and drink wine
Root work and drink wine
Make love and drink wine
But she don't cook nuthin fo nobody
Erybody know bout dat

Ms. Isidore lookin real good for her age
She shoal like to flirt
When Ma Chevery out fishin
She say I's a handsome woman
I's jus like my daddy
Ms. Isidore like women and like mules
Seasoned and dependable
I ain't either, yet
Erybody know bout dat

Ms. Isidore love Ma Chevery
Ms. Isidore love her mules too
Specially the one her daddy gave her
Magic Black Isidore been dead at least forty years
The mule an old good boy
His name been Marian Anderson
Since the first day
He don't mind it one bit

Ms. Isidore love Ma Chevery and Marian Anderson
She call em both Ma
With the same tenderness
She love em more than she could

Say to em or bout em
Erybody know bout dat

III. MARDI GRAS KITCHEN

Ms. Isidore, Dauphine, and the ladies
Carryin on in the kitchen
Sewing gowns and pressing hair
Kings and queens and courts and parades
Balls all weekend
Mass on Sunday
Mardi Gras gumbo
King cake on Tuesday

I ain't bout to go nowhere
Dressed up like the pope
I's jus like my daddy
He don't go nowheres for nothing
Cept to visit ladyfriends
Cept a repast after the funeral
Of somebody humble
Cept Blessin of the Shrimp fleet

I ain't thinkinbout nobody's Mardi Gras
Cept maybe thinkinbout up under Dauphine's gown she gon
    wear
bout moss and salt water and hurricanes under her slip
Don't nobody ask what I know bout dat

Ladies primpin and fussin
Can't find the parasol in the closet
Mrs. Tillman say it betta not be in the toolshed
With the fishing tackle and umbrellas
Mamma Dear get worked up
She say parasol ain't no umbrella
Say she like to see my daddy

Walkin round in the rain with all that lace trim
She put on it

Dey all fall out laughin
Ms. Isidore even spill half her wine
Down her bosom
Mamma Dear can hear
In her left ear
A little
If she can get in a joke on my daddy
Hear laughter
Even though she don't hear nothing
She don't wanna to hear

I ain't goin in the kitchen
Dey gon poke fun and try da get me up in a gown
Just ta see if I'm as pretty as I am handsome
Dey know itaintright
Dauphine can jus tellem
Yes
Cause she know bout dat

IV. DAUPHINE
I whisper to Dauphine through the screen back door
Latched with a hook from the inside
Pssssssst
Pass me some Moon Pies off the counter
She suck her teeth at me
Sccccccth
She roll her eyes
She latched herself with a hook from the inside

I ask please, I say sorry
I mean it
She blush

She wink
She grin
She put her hands on her hips
She unlatch the door
She unlatch her smile

She tell me go check on her crab traps
She put down
In the bayou with two chicken necks this morning
She give me some half-melted moon pies out her pocket
She latch the screen door back
She latch her lips back
She turn her back but don't walk away
We still feelin through the screen

V. MISS KATRINA
Aeyo!
I got us some moon pies Miss Katrina
I yell out to the bayou
Now don't nobody think catfish can hear you talkin
That's just cus they ain't tried talkin to em
Catfish got ears bout like ours you know, and plenty sense too
Aeyo!

Miss Katrina come out the mud slow
She swim to me and lift the fin on her back
She float on her side
And look at me with her toolittle blue eye
The same toosmall blue eyes Mrs. Tillman's
Tubby brown baby got
Erybody know bout dat

Miss Katrina keep me company
While I pull the traps and see what crabs
We got to put in de

Mardi Gras gumbo
They still dancing and fiddling and pinchin each other
Over what left of the chicken necks

Miss Katrina eat anything cept what's on a hook
And Mrs. Valerie's potato salad
Jus like anybody
who got sense
who got the will to live
Once I gave her some'that potato salad on a spoon
jus to see
Miss Katrina spat
Went back in the mud over that
She ain't come out til I gave her
A quarter pound of bait shrimp to apologize

I named her after the storm
When the Bayou changed
That's when she came to stay
In the bend
In our yard
She as big and the color of Mamma Dear's thigh
With housecoat hiked up high
In the afternoon heat

I sink down in the bayou
Open the moon pie wrappers
Lemme see Miss Katrina
You like marshmallow
Chocolate or vanilla?
Miss Katrina Catfish Mardi Gras Queen
She like chocolate moon pie too

Miss Katrina make kisses at me
She got long whiskers like

Granddaddy Beau's photo in the foyer
And bout as friendly
No teeth in dey smile
Miss Katrina got on red lipstick
Like what my daddy got on him when he come home
After kissin
And he don't know bout it

I's just like my daddy
Dis said and meant all kindaways

Bayou Honeyman

Honeyman live freer than erybody else.

Honeyman appear and disappear, somewhere between Satsuma and Creola, between Mon Louis Island and Bayou Coden. Don't nobody know which creek Honeyman live on, ain't nobody goin lookin. Erybody think on what Honeyman do when they can't see whatitis. Honeyman like a riverboat coming in and leavin out at the same time.

Honeyman bring jars down the river, a woven basket in the crook of Honeyman's arm. Honeyman a bee, round and sharp and spindly at the same time. Erybody like Honeyman's sweet. Erybody wonder why they drawn to Honeyman when they can't think whatitis. Honeyman walk slow and hum low, erybody feel Honeyman's sound climbing round in their ribs' hive.

Bette like Honeyman, she run up a cloud of red clay. She like to be first to see Honeyman come round the river bend. Bette clap her hands and point her toes, she meet Honeyman on Chickasaw Creek and sit in the boat for a ways. Bette sing and talk at Honeyman, she sigh, she show her neck. Bette fold and unfold herself, rocking the boat side to side. She bring a few pieces of pie to taste. Honeyman like a slice of pie.

Georgewaters like Honeyman, he take a jar out the basket and blush. Georgewaters stare deep at Honeyman, get low humming back. Georgewaters sweat and fidget. He get brave, invite Honeyman skinnydippin in the cold swimming hole. Georgewaters unscrew the honey top, stick his finger in the jar to taste. Georgewaters like a basted ham when Honeyman bring jars down the river. Honeyman like basted ham.

Honeyman love Leticia, she prop open her back door with a jug of whisky when it rains. She play music and wait on the steps in her slip. Leticia braid and unbraid her hair. Leticia smoke tobacco in a pipe. Leticia walk around in high-heel shoes and panties in the house. Leticia leave the windows open, cept when Honeyman come. Erybody already know, Leticia love Honeyman and a jug of whisky.

I love Honeyman, I skip in a circle, I squeal, I bounce. Muh'deah call me, "Honeybaby you raising the dead with that racket." She threaten the cake in the oven we made for Honeyman bout to fall. Mydaddy Beau call me, "Honeybaby, come sit still." He hand me a cool glass of water, he rock me in the rocking chair with his foot. Mydaddy Beau love Honeyman, been lookin out from the porch all day. Mydaddy Beau got to wait til just one jar left. Mydaddy Beau love a jar of honey.

Honeyman come down the road, hum, slow. I can feel Honeyman's hum between my shoulders' hive. Honeyman like a riverboat coming in and leavin out at the same time. Mydaddy Beau run out to the road and take Honeyman's basket, take Honeyman's hand. I race, I jump, I cling, I hold Honeyman round the neck. I sit on Honeyman's hip. I look in Honeyman's mirror, I'm a bee, round and sharp and spindly at the same time. Muh'deah call me to the kitchen, "Honeybaby, fix yo'mamma Honeyman a plate."

Honeyman call me, "Honeybaby, I save the last jar of honey for you every time."

Water Recipe

Ma'muh what you fixin'a cook?
Water

Prep time

Hesh chile my stories bout to come on—till—papa come home
from fishin'

Servings: All y'all

Ingredients

1 yellow green and pink floral
    housecoat
Undergarments (slip optional)
1 jar of green DAX Pomade
2 spritzes of Chantilly Eau De
    Toilette
A bit of chilren gigglin' bout
    "ewwwwwwww, the toilet!"
Fresh blue house shoes embroi-
    dered with red roses
1 tattered red flyswatter
5 to 7 medium-sized white potatoes

Fresh parsley (cut real fine)
4 stalks of celery (yellow, try not
    to get the green kind)
1 medium-sized onion
3 green onions (tops and all)
1 large bell pepper
Blue Plate Mayonnaise
1 jar of salad pickles
Black pepper
All season
7 boiled eggs (save 2 for the top)

Ma'muh what you cookin?
Water

Boil water

Follow precise measurements

Let the phone ring two times
    before pickin up
"Lewis residence, Arvilla speakin."
    (muddled greeting)
"Hey there Tila, howyou?"
    (muddled chatter)
"Um hm, well, I'm jus
    finna cook…" (muddled
    chatter)

"Yes, um hm, ummmm, umph
    ump umph!" (muddled gossip)
"She done tole me, um, ummm
    hmmm" (muddled gossip)
"What you say, umph!" (muddled
    gossip)
"Well, rain shoal is wet, ain't it!"
    (muddled laughter)
Laugh til your sides hurt

Preparation

Step 1
Ma'muh what you cookin?
Water

Boil water

Cook potatoes til a fork will slip in and out easily
Drain potatoes
Remove and let potatoes cool
Peel potatoes
Cube potatoes

Step 2
Fetch Ollie out of oak tree tops
Wash Ollie's hands and arms
Pour witch hazel on Ollie's skint'up knee
Dab pink calamine on Ollie's mosquito bites

Remove amphibians and insecta *Arthropoda* from Ollie's
   pockets
Place Ollie's magni-fine glass in the bottom drawer of the
   apothecary pantry
Place Ollie's Farmers' Almanac on the Singer sewing machine
Tie Ollie's hair up with a blue ribbon
Set Ollie to cut parsley, celery, onion, and green onion
Wipe Ollie's tears with a clean white hanker'chief
Add cut vegetables to potatoes
Add jar of salad pickles
Add mayonnaise (use enough to make the salad so that it is not
   stiff)
Mix with hands
Send Ollie back outside til dinner is served
Place bowl in the fridgerator

Step 3

Gradually ascend the staircase to the bedroom
Turn on the Westinghouse Whirlwind fan on the dresser
Open window, threaten to whip boisterous children for chasing
   the cat
Repeat "Lawd these children"
Shake head
Pull lace curtains (but let them blow)
Discard yellow and pink floral housecoat
Keep undergarments (slip optional)
Pray rosary
Lay acrost'de bed for a spell

Step 4

Rise
Pour cool water into washbowl from pitcher
Splash water on face, neck, and arms
Dry with a clean cloth

Dress in fresh supportive undergarments and slip (to modestly
   mold the body)
Dress in purple housecoat
Gradually descend the staircase

Step 5

Remove bowl from the fridgerator
Add jar of salad pickles
Add black pepper to taste
Add all season to taste
Taste

Step 6

Ma'muh what you cookin?
Water

Boil water

Cook 7 eggs hard-boiled
Remove and let eggs cool
Peel eggs
Save two eggs
Slice remaining eggs and stir into potato salad
Cut remaining eggs in rounds
Place rounds on the top of the potato salad

Step 7

Wash dishes
Prepare kitchen for dessert preparation

Dessert

Prep time

Chile come set this table—til dinner bell

Servings

Pappa'nem

Ingredients

2 uncles, 1 priest (Father Lundi, preferable), and papa come home from fishin

Ant' Rosetta (optional)

Fresh cool late afternoon breeze off the Gulf

11 camellias in a mason jar bouquet left on the porch by Ms. Lorraine

Radio to taste

8 large sweet potatoes

7 large eggs (be sure to add them last)

4 cups of sugar

1 lb and 1 stick of Land O Lakes Margarine

1 can of Carnation condensed milk (use ½ to start, you can add more to get right texture)

Lemon flavor to taste

Vanilla flavor to taste

Nutmeg to taste

Allspice to taste

Cinnamon to taste Taste

Juice from 2 real lemons

½ cup of flour to thicken (sift so it will be fine, it will help with the browning)

Ma'muh what you cookin?
Water

Boil water

Follow precise measurements

Open window to observe

"Ollie, I done tole you not to mess with my cat!" (muddled denial)

"Why Tony got a whole clump of fur missing off his backside, then?" (muddled excuse)

"That cat ain't no science 'spearmint!" (muddled justification)

"Leave Tony 'lone, ya'heard" (muddled whimper involving "felis catus *Domesticus* examination")

"T'ain't gonna tell you again" (muddled acceptance)

"Now hesh up that cryin and come gimme some sugar" (sniffles, then chuckles)

Preparation

Step 1
Ma'muh what you cookin?
Water

Boil water

Cook sweet potatoes til a fork will slip in and out easily
Drain sweet potatoes (if you don't they will be watery)
Remove and let sweet potatoes cool
Peel sweet potatoes

Step 2
Fetch Asberry from under the house
Wash red clay from around Asberry's mouth, face, and hands
Inspect Asberry's tongue
Check Asberry's nose
Remove moss from Asberry's hair
Procure Asberry a clean shirt and shorts
Fetch Edna and dispense of Asberry
Ensure Edna obtains a modest garment to cover her shoulders
Measure Edna's skirt to taste
Prepare Edna to set the table

Step 3
Beat peeled sweet potatoes (this will take the strings out)
Add all other ingredients (be sure to add eggs last)

Add mixture to pie crust (only make your own pie crust on
    Sundays after mass)
Preheat the oven to 400
Cook crust and pie together (do not cook crust first)
Remove sweet potato pie from the oven
Set aside to cool

Ring the dinner bell

A note of thanks

I would like to thank my grandmother, Clara Nell, for these recipes
and my mother for transcribing them exactly as her mother-in-law
told them to her. I'd also like to thank Edna Lewis for her recipes,
stories, and inspiration. May my Granddaddy Lewis's cat Tony rest
in peace.

Praise Song for Blue Crab

Crab es'the dainty fiddler
Crab mumbles bubbles into the sea breeze
On many legs, dancing
Hastening, to the taste of decay

Crab deep blue, twists and folds
Legs held tight
To white underside
Into steel wire, delicious contraption

Crab who feasts and fusses
Worry to death
Others as they pluck, chicken neck from the mesh
Win esteemed position, pull the meat

Crab removed from trap
Scuttle and pose
Claws raised to the sun
An invitation to pinch

Crab in bucket
Thrashing and scaling
Kin beneath and below
Hoisting to freedom

Crab over the bucket lip
Onto the deck, over the side
Splash of water sings
Crab claws are yours tonight

PART 2

Fire

Recipe River. Digital photograph by Mel Michelle Lewis, 2023.

Elemental Essay: Fire

My voice is fire. How does fire speak?

Living Fire

My people have a relationship with fire. It is revered in ways that are ancient, the cooking fire, the warming fire, the illuminating fire. It is also feared in ways that are corporeal. My people have a relationship with destructive fire; home ablaze, bodies burned, smoke-last-breath-fire. Fire is a protective prayer and a religious ritual. Fire is sanctified.

My people have prayed with fire, lived in fire, lived on fire, died in fire. The constant touch of fire:

Cook blister
Sun burn
Curl singe
Ember scorch
Pot scald
House blaze

There is only one way with fire. Keep going. In *Parable of the Sower*, Octavia Butler writes of this way through fire:

> There was nothing to do except keep going or burn. The terrible, deafening noise of the fire increased, then lessened, and again,

increased, then lessened. . . . Like a tornado of fire, roaring around, just missing us, playing with us, then letting us live.[1]

Fire is always "playing with us," and sometimes, it does not let us live, on this side. Some of us are smolder, on the other side of fire. Evie Shockley offers another critical assertion in her poem "playing with fire":

> something is always burning, passion,
>   pride, envy, desire, the internal organs
> going chokingly up in smoke, as some-
>   thing outside the body exerts a pull
> that drags us like a match across sand-
>   paper.[2]

We are dragged matches.

My father grew up in Toulminville, in the 1950s just across from what is now the Henry Aaron Park, near Threemile Creek. Henry Aaron (don't call him Hank!) of baseball fame was his babysitter. Previously called Bayou Chateauguay, Threemile Creek is known as the baptism site for survivors of the *Clotilda* and Africatown's descendants. Flowing between the Mobile River at Magazine Point through the heart of Mobile, it runs for fourteen miles. Threemile is named for its confluence "three miles north" of the river's mouth at Mobile Bay, not its length. Today the creek is so polluted its use designation is only industrial.

> Don't drink
> The firewater
> Don't touch
> The waterfire

During my father's childhood, my grandparent's Toulminville house caught fire. My grandmother was severely burned. My father's sister, "Auntie Bunny," age eleven, died in the fire. This shaped my relationship with my grandmother, "Muh'deah" Clara Nell Lewis, and with the element fire. My Muh'deah knew me and her daughter, Bunny, as the same being. Fire let Bunny live, ignited in me. As Shockley writes, "something is always burning." I admit this has been a difficult element to allow to speak through me; it has singed and blistered, but it has also cauterized and healed. I am particularly grateful for Muh'deah's flame, illuminating my way through the narratives of fire.

Wearing Fire

My illuminated memory sees Muh'deah, Clara Nell Lewis, donning her housecoats. She wore fire. After wearing fire, wearing housecoats was an act of liberation for Muh'deah, particularly in her cultural context and time, which demanded a highly curated "respectable" feminine aesthetic "of prominence" in the community. I see Muh'deah's act of self-care to be political and powerful. Black feminist scholar Tanisha C. Ford's text *Liberated Threads: Black Women, Style, and the Global Politics of Soul* explores this act; she writes: "I uncover how and why Black women incorporated dress into their activist strategies. Body politics assumed many forms as black women across the diaspora fought to define their dressed bodies on their own terms."[3] Muh'deah existed on her own terms.

Although Muh'deah was a devout Catholic, working-class family woman, cook, seer, healer, and bayou fisherwoman, she also had a politics of "up-in-de-house" fashion and beauty product regimen. In her early thirties, with seven children to care for, she suffered major burns to the entirety of her body in the house fire. She received the treatment available to Black women in segregated coastal Alabama in the early 1950s, skin grafts, perhaps advanced by WWII medical innovations, but quite extensive and painful. I situate her process of care and healing in the context of Alabama's racist medical history. Janell Hobson, in *Body as Evidence: Mediating Race, Globalizing Gender*, writes:

> Experiments were performed on enslaved women, including Anarcha and Lucy, whose bodies fueled the early work of J. Marion Sims in Alabama from 1840 to 1849 . . . the legacy of scientific objectification and dehumanization of black bodies. Such acts would later reverberate in the horrific example of the Tuskegee experiments, which subjected black men in Alabama, who went untreated for syphilis, to medical experimentation for scientific study between 1932 and 1972.[4]

Due to her medical conditions, including light, heat, and chemical sensitivities, during my youth Muh'deah almost never left the house other than for a one-hour mass on Sundays. For mass she wore her undergarments, girdle, pantyhose, skirt suit, heels, brooch, and red lipstick, shaping her very long wavy salt-and-pepper hair—which never went fully gray during her lifetime—into slick ringlets with a giant jar of green DAX Pomade, which always had a rusty metal top from the bathroom moisture and the salty sea air coming through the open windows.

Other than that one fully clothed hour per week, Muh'deah's body politic and liberated threads included what I believe were hundreds of soft floral housecoats, with snaps down the front. Light ones or heavy ones depending on the weather, holiday theme prints for Christmas, Easter, and Fourth of Ju'ly, and sometimes patterns to incorporate any stains that might occur depending on the household menu for the day.

Loving Fire

I'm not sure what else was under those housecoats, other than her round, bare, blonde, patchwork body covered in cocoa butter lotion and the hint of Chantilly perfume, the only perfume which did not cause her chemical sensitivities to flare up. Muh'deah's liberated threads housecoat-couture gave a refuge for her burned body and were worn in stark contrast to my grandfather's gaze. As she floated around the kitchen in her purple hydrangea patterns, Grandaddy Lewis would comment that he usta'could tie his handkerchief around her waist when they were courting. Seven children and more than sixty years later, she would turn down the fire on the stove, pull out the chair next to him at the kitchen table. Muh'deah would hike her housecoat up over her knees and sit down next to him, pouring all of her roundness over his butter biscuits and Karo Corn Syrup ham. She would pretend to be vexed, and he would pretend to be indignant, then they would bust out laughing, both with their dentures in napkins on the table.

Although they did not share a bedroom in our shared home during my childhood, I now recognize the evidence of intimacy, perhaps even passion, in those moments between my grandparents, touched by fire and loss. In her book *Eloquent Rage: A Black Feminist Discovers Her Superpower*, Britney Cooper wishes the same laughter for us, noting, "When we lack joy, we have diminished our capacity for self-love and self-valuing and for empathy" and wishes for us, "may you have gut-busting laughter every day."[5] Although there are smoke and fire in this elemental section, there are also sparks of laughter and fluttering joyful flames.

Writing Fire

The element fire is reflective; my memory and imagination are ignited. The first section, "Tongues of Fire," is a reading from the book of my childhood memories. In this narrative self-portrait, the Black Creole Catholic context intersects with my queer coming of age and my feminist politic. The second entry in this section, "Twin Flames on the Other Side of Fire," is a meditation on Ancestors who live through and within us. This narrative is both familial and ceremonial; I dedicate this work to the little Auntie Bunny in me.

Next, "Ashy" reveals winter skin as a respite from humidity and heaviness, no matter the searing discomfort. Engaging the post–Hurricane Katrina milieu of coastal Alabama, "Ceasefire" offers insight into labor, love, and heroic mundane Black queer coastal living. I close the element fire with a jazz poem, conjuring the lucky and the hapless in New Orleans, Biloxi, and Mobile. "Jazz Fired" is dedicated to the jazz poets as well as deep gratitude for the style and spirit of Gwendolyn Brooks.

Fire Invocation for the Reader

May you know the presence of fire
Warm hearth
Heart ablaze
May you know the absence of fire
Ashes at rest
Extinguished in peace
May you know the presence of fire
Incandescence
Ancestral Amen Ashé

Filé Sassafras. Digital photograph by Mel Michelle Lewis, 2023.

Tongues of Fire

I. SUNDAY MORNIN'
Light a candle
Pray bout it

Mother have Rose wake me up
Extra early on Sunday mornin'
Mother been up before dawn
Pray rosary on the pier
Even though we bout to go to church
Mother a nervous bayou mouse
Cache of prayers in the seagrass

Rose pull covers off me
Rose plead and appeal
Rose put up with my sleepy slow
Rose is delicate petals and full sun
Don't know how much
Rose paid to
Love us
But she
Love me
Some her ownself for free
I think

Mother have Rose part my hair
Comb
Elongate
Grease
Saturate
Pull
Control
Braid
Harness
Band
Restrain!

Make two tight pigtail braids
Use bands with the colorful
Hard plastic balls
Crack me in the tooth
Pop me in the eye
If I play too much

Pigtail braids stand out

Balls on the top
Pink
Taut
Balls on the bottom
Blue
Swing

Light a candle
Pray bout it

Mother have Rose dress me in
Lace. Itchy
Tights. Itchy
Crinolines. ITCHY.

I stand out

Mother have Rose iron dress shirts
Fold underclothes
Hang dry-cleaning ensembles
Make cheese toast
Grits and scrambled eggs
Wash dishes

THE CHIEF wake up
Just in time on Sunday morning
Splash in the tub
A brown pelican gentleman
Groom tidy
Smell good
THE CHIEF emerge from the bathroom
Fully clothed in a three-piece suit and hard shoes
Never half-dressed

THE CHIEF sing, "Greetings my daughter"
THE CHIEF sing, "You can be beautiful too"
We laugh, together
But is it true?

Light a candle
Pray bout it

Mother go get in the car
When she ready
To go
To mass
Sit. Alone. And wait
Smolder

Don't be late
Won't be late

THE CHIEF emerge from the kitchen
Just in time
THE CHIEF say, "Well mercy be"
Mother have Rose sit me still
In the back seat

II. MASS MEMORY
Genuflect
Show respect

I dip two fingers
Into the cool water
Cross myself
Dab
Like perfume
Forehead Heart Shoulder Shoulder
Father Son Holy Spirit

The sanctuary is
Obedient ablaze
Candles
Flames
Licking the spirit air
Gentle
Reverent
Mother and THE CHIEF whisper
Shake hands embrace parishioners

Devout adults adore devout children
I adore adoration
I wave
I curtsy
I hug
Parishioners whisper and smile

"Peace be with you"
I croon "and also with you"

I am "a pretty little thing"
I am "a blessing"
I am "precious, clean, well behaved, darling"
They love me
Jesus loves me
Yes I know

The priest parade
Enters
I am ecstatic
Bells and smoke and singing
Blessings and vestments and burning
Flames
Body of Christ

Genuflect
Show respect

I'd ask what time it is, but
Sayeth the Lord
Don'chu neva eva
"upon the wicked he shall rain snares, fire and brimstone, and a
    horrible tempest, this shall be the portion of their cup"
If I ask

I'd slip out of my too-tight patent leather shoes, but
Jesus answered
Umph, what ya oughttado'es
"obey your parents in all things, for this is well pleasing unto the
    Lord"
I shan't take them off

I'd say I need to go to the bathroom, but
The Lord revealed unto thee
Nauh uh, itaintright
"Honor thy father and thy mother"
Do not interrupt

I'd loosen my pigtails, but
The Lord sayeth
You betta not, chile
"We believe in one God the Father almighty, maker of heaven
    and earth"
I can't let them loose

I'd scratch my legs cocooned in itchy tights, but
Behold, said the Lord thy God
You betta set'down and halt thy fidgeting
"Lest ye face eternal damnation"
I won't budge just in case

I'd ask if we can get French toast sticks at Burger King after
    mass, but
"Pray for us sinners, now and at the hour of our death"
I'll wait till someone else wants
What I want

I'd lay down on the pew for a nap, but
"Jesus wept"

The priest parade
Exits
I am ecstatic
Bells and smoke and singing
Blessings and vestments and burning
Flames
Body of Christ

III. 1993 NEWS
It's on the news
Catholic Church rules in favor of allowing girl altar servers

It's on the news
Hawaii rules limiting marriage to opposite-sex couples is
    unconstitutional

Allowed

Girls
Will be
Allowed to be altar boys
Girls
Will not be
Allowed to be priests
But
Girls
Will be
Allowed to be altar boys

Queers
Will be
Allowed to be.

I will be an altar boy
Will I be a priest?
Sayeth the Lord thy God, "Behold, I am doing a new
    thing! Now it springs up; do you not perceive it? I am
    making a way in the wilderness and streams in the
    wasteland."

I am the
Cross Bearer
I set the chalice

I hold the missal
I am the fire that lights the holy candles
I ring the bells
Under flowing vestments I am
Eucharist body and blood

I want to give the homily
Study
Read
Write
Learn
Teach
Inspire
Serve
Comfort

Allowed

I meet with the priest
To discuss being a priest
Girls
Will not be
Allowed to be priests

I meet with the priest
To discuss being a queer
Holy Mary
Mother of God!

IV. 1995 SACRAMENT
I wear a long loose braid and a bandanna
I wear cargo shorts and a rainbow tie-dye T-shirt
In the style of the Grateful Dead
With more benign bears
My Catholic Junior High School's

Spirit day design on the back
"GRATEFUL Jesus has risen from the DEAD"

I am to be confirmed
I wait on the steps
For the parish service van
To take me to do community service
I am to be confirmed

I wonder if
This is how nuns
Are presented
To a convent
I wonder if
This is how queers
Get committed
To an asylum

The Priest likes
To ask me
What I want to do with
Girls
I don't know much
Hold hands
Pray
The Priest likes
To tell me there are other things
Pentecost
Tongues of fire
Blessed assurance

I have not yet considered
A prayer
for tongues

Upon me
Now do

Everyone
Not Mother and THE CHIEF
Has suggested
I think about being a nun
Girls
Will not be
Allowed to be priests

Everyone
Not Mother and THE CHIEF
Has an inkling
I want to do what nuns do
In a convent

I have no idea
What nuns do
In a convent
Wash each other's feet with tears
Anoint with ointment
Dry with their hair

Absolution

I think about being a nun
I have an
Aunt-in-law and cousin nuns
Immaculate women

No one my age wants to be a
Nun
Priest

Catholic
No one my age wants to be a
Prude
Slut
Queer

The parish service van drives me
To the Dominican Monastery of St. Jude
To do service
I expect to be left
Girls
Will not be
Allowed to be priests

Sister Dominican Monastery of St. Jude
Invites me in
Sister Dominican Monastery of St. Jude
Instructs me

Light a candle
Pray bout it

Sister Dominican Monastery of St. Jude
And her Sisters
Have not seen the sun in generations
I don't think I am old enough
To be a nun

I am instructed to
Take the basket
Pick up sticks
In the courtyard
Kindling
For the fire

After finding out
More about nuns
I decide
To find out
More about myself

Queers
Will be
Allowed to
Be.

Twin Flames on the Other Side of Fire

I. TWIN FLAMES

We got a few sets of identical twins in the family
Siblings are two people who share the same parents
Twins are
The same person two times
Twins are
The same person two times

Nobody arguebout the possibility of living
More than once at the same time
When they call
Un'cle Cletus and Un'cle Rufus
To fix
The shrimp boat motor
The backhoe tractor

No one say it's sacrilegious to exist
Twice simultaneously
When they ask
Cousin May and Cousin Fay
To fix
The pound cake
The lemon pie

No one say you tellin a story
When Big Pappy and Ole Fats
Play like
They both at the cookout
They both at the reunion
Ain't but one
Eatin seconds
Again

Ain't no flyin off the handle bout that
Ain't no hesh yo mouth bout that
Ain't no carryin on bout that
We got a few sets of identical twins in the family

There's a difference
Between most folks
And the mirror
There's a difference
Between most folks
Awake and in a dream
There's a difference
Between most folks
Who died before and
Who was born after

But, we ain't most folks

Lapine live on the other side of fire

Her parents are my grandparents
Our people
Her brother is my father
Our people
They still on this side of fire

There's no word I'm allowed to say
For kin who
The same person two times
The same person two times
That was dead and is alive
The way I am alive
The way I am alive

There's no word I'm allowed to say
For kin who
The same body
With the same spirit
Not like being possessed by the Devil
Just
Being the same person that was another person
At the same time that
I am
Another person who is the same person
Just
Being the same person that was another person
At the same time that
I am
Another person who is the same person

Lapine live on the other side of fire

II. ON THE OTHER SIDE OF FIRE
Mamma Isidore know what we are
She call us Lapine just as often
As she call us Dauphine
She see through we
She look at we
At the same time
At the same time

Erybody say
Mamma Isidore was burned
Erybody say
Her mind took smoke
Mix things up
Erybody say
She been mourning
Over fifty years
Erybody say
She can't help it
She ain't the same person that she used to be
She ain't the same person that she used to be

Mamma Isidore show us how to
Clean fish
Again
Plait hair
Again
Make biscuits
Again
Make gumbo
Again
Tie a sash ribbon in back
Again
Bake red velvet cake
Again
She know
I know
She done showed we
She done showed we
When I was her lil'gal

Ma'am don't like one bit
Mamma Isidore calling us lil'gal or Lapine
She politely pry us from Mamma Isadore

Send us

Go fetch the stuff, "yes Ma'am"

Go put the thing over yonder, "yes Ma'am"

Bring me the thing, no, the other thing, hmm um, no, the other
thing, "yes Ma'am"

Go fetch the stuff and set it next to the thing over yonder, "yes
Ma'am"

Go see about ___, "yes Ma'am"

Go ask ___, "yes Ma'am"

Go tell ___, "yes Ma'am"

A wild goose chase

A fool's errand

Practice adding and subtracting, "yes Ma'am"

Practice vocabulary, "yes Ma'am"

Practice cursive handwriting, "yes Ma'am"

Practice your needlepoint, "yes Ma'am"

Practice piano, "yes Ma'am"

We don't have no piano

Ma'am know what we are

But afraid ise the Devil

I look just like myself

The spit'in image

Ma'am hide the Lapine photo in the foyer

Put up another Dauphine photo in its place

Somebody always notice and

Put it back before sundown on Sunday

Don't know whoitis

Ma'am think ise me

I'd tell her it ain't

But if ise Lapine

Then it ise me

And the Devil is a lie
So I ain't say nuthin

Daddy know what we are
I'm sisterdaughter
This give us all troubletrouble
Daddy and we love uneasy
Daddy bring us penny candy
Watch with big eyes and turn away
Daddy scold us nicely
Then we both crycry
We don't have no siblings
Cept big brotherdaddy
Daddy get small and hold my hand
Like he done held my hand
Like he done held my hand
When I was lil'gal

Lapine live on the other side of fire

Give Daddy nightmares
Remembering the burning
Give Daddy cold sweats
Remembering the burning
He can feel that I know
I know
Mamma Isadore give Daddy an
Acifidity bag to hang round his neck
Ma'am know what it is
But afraid ise the Devil
She slip it off his neck when he
Sleep in the rocking chair
Say she can't stand the smell
Of burning

Winter come round and we got Lapine Birthday
Summer come round and we got Dauphine Birthday
Winter birthday folks solemn
All cept Mamma Isadore
And we

The family gathers and whispers
Big Pappy and Old Fats
The fire
Before the fire
In the fire
After the fire
Cousin May and Cousin Fay
The fire
Before the fire
In the fire
After the fire

The fire

On Lapine Birthday
Mamma Isadore
And we
Justcookin and a carrin'on
She got a laugh that'll raise the dead
Round noon folks walk slow down the dirt path
To the graves
Of those in the ground
For now

Place flowers for our birthday
I place a bouquet for we
And giggle with Mamma Isadore

About all the flowers
About all the flowers
The old folks ought'ta tell me hesh up
The old folks ought'ta tell me stop playin
But on Lapine Birthday, don't nobody bother we
They all cut their eyes at we
Forget to breathe

On Dauphine Birthday
Ma'am fret over our every move
Make us up into a doll
Lifelike
Sing a song Dauphine, "yes Ma'am"
Mamma Isadore get to laughin and slappin her thigh
Do a dance Dauphine, "yes Ma'am"
Mamma Isadore full on laughin and clappin
Recite a poem Dauphine, "yes Ma'am"
Mamma Isadore laugh so hard she fall out the chair
Got to be raised up

We eat cake
No candles
No flame
No wishes
Just prayers
For a long life

Ashy

Hearth knees
Genuflect sticks
Fireside dry

Pondering elbow
Chin listening
Radio rustle

Hollow lotion
Fishing stick
Skin sip

Bayou winter
Crust stare
Nose tartar

Pomade essence
Fingernail scrape
Straw curl

Pecan sandies
Desiccated skins
Knuckle snow

Heel hole
Darn socks
Toe hide

Prayer knit
Peppermint lick
Lip split

Seer sear
Ashes ashes
Dust dust

Ceasefire

Erybody got trash to burn.
PyroBeau come round every mornin in an ole rusty truck. He got gloves, a shovel, and a wheelbarrow. Fine-lookin like an ole snapping turtle, stocky, wrinkled, heroic. Jus'bout every day PyroBeau come by, he splain it, "Ain't no municipal pickup, ya see? Ain't no other way, ya see? Ima take care of it, ya see, for a small fee." It's good to splain things to folk, specially folk who got trash.

Erybody got trash to burn.
PyroBeau wear heavy work gloves; ain't nobody seen his hands to know if he really got any. Some folks whisper bout his glovehands, "Veet'Nham," when he came back . . . how he came back . . . that he came back. PyroBeau take a cool glass of water with lemon, or sweet tea, if'n you offer him some. He obliged, "Thank'ye much." PyroBeau hold the glass with just his thumb and forefinger, send it down, then sigh out loud and long, "ahhhhhhhhhhh!" He don't take off them gloves. He eat a biscuit or a tea cake, if'n you offer him some. He real thankful, "I shoal do preciate it." PyroBeau flip the cake off the saucer onto his glovehand, then open wide and flip it into his turtle mouth. He chew and hand back the saucer, "Mmmmmm mmmm mph!" He don't take off them gloves.

Erybody got trash to burn.
Once he got a full ole rusty truck, PyroBeau drive down to the docks. Coosa hear that truck growlin down the drive, he clock out

and take off in a sprint. Coosa like a back bay flounder: free, flat, funny. Coosa look like he got a long luscious white Mardi Gras wig on, like the ones with the soft curls in the boutique window. It just grow out his head like that; he keep it so pretty.

PyroBeau and Coosa got a ritual. PyroBeau pull up to the boat launch, he reach acrost the seat and roll down the window, he call out, "Hay'dah." Coosa wave at him fluttering his fingers fast a real long time with one hand and hold up an ice-cold can of Co'Cola in the other hand from the corroded pier vending machine. Coosa get in the ole rusty truck and offer PyroBeau a cigarette out the pack in his shirt pocket. PyroBeau smile and wink. Coosa smile and wink. They both got nice teeth for their age, don't nobody know how. Coosa lean acrost the seat and light the cigarette for PyroBeau, then lean back on the door, watching. PyroBeau take a few long drags then hand the half cigarette back. Coosa finish it off and flip it out the window. PyroBeau pop open the cold Co'Cola, hand the can to Coosa who gulp down the top third. Coosa say, "Heah, you wan'some?" PyroBeau take a sip or two to wet his whistle. He like to let Coosa drink the rest. PyroBeau peel out down the dirt road.

Erybody got trash to burn.
PyroBeau and Coosa pull off the road. They live on Bayou Coden, way back. They towed the FEMA trailer off the paved street a few years ago, kept it; lots of folks did. PyroBeau splain, "Ain't no sense in doing right by FEMA, ya see? It ain't even stealing, the way they did us, ya see? Sposedtabe toxic, but ain't no more toxic than erydae, ya see? It ain't nuthin fa'me, ya see?" Coosa do get nose-bleeds sometimes, but he splain, "I had those all my life, on account'a bein high-strung, leas das'how my Mamma Coosa wud'tellit." Coosa never miss a time ta'tell PyroBeau what Mamma Coosa usetasay.

PyroBeau drive the truck out to the clearing, where Coosa set up the fifty-five-gallon drums he brought for PyroBeau from off the docks. Before they get to unloading, PyroBeau pull out a little trinket or tidbit he set aside for Coosa, hold it out with his glovehand clenched, then slowly open his fingers to reveal the treasure. PyroBeau smile and wink. Coosa smile and wink. Coosa love it, fix it, wear it, use it, make something for somebody with it. Something somebody just threw away.

Erybody got trash to burn.
Coosa help PyroBeau unload the trash into the 55-gallon drum. PyroBeau pour himself a mason jar of gasoline, he douse, he light a match, he flick it with his glovehand. Coosa like that part. He stay for the lighting, then drive the ole rusty truck back to the docks to clockin. PyroBeau watch the burn. He stoke, regulate, extinguish escaping embers. He pace slowly around the inferno in a circle like a shark, moving closer as the smoke shifts. A dance. A ceremony. A cremation. For all the things, didn't nobody want, didn't nobody need no more. Erybody need PyroBeau, though, ya see? Folks at war with their own refuse.

Zora Menagerie. Digital photograph by Mel Michelle Lewis, 2023.

Jazz Fired

Jazz play
    On bourbon day
Make love
    With fallen dove
Catfish Fry
    Little white lie

Get fired.

Alabama Port
    A dollar short
Biloxi bound
    House burn down
Play the horn
    Baby born

Get fired.

Oyster shuck
    Lunch break fuck
Cuss a fool
    Follow the rule
Shrimp po'boy
    Gurl act coy

Get fired.

Sip wine
    Invite to dine
Rosary pray
    Sleep all day
Bet racetrack
    Don't pay back

Get fired.

Mississippi sound
    Crawfish pound
Gig offshore
    Baton Rouge tour
Shimmy dance
    Final last chance

Get fired.

Riverboat float
    No bank note
Beau Rivage
    Econo Lodge
Get a rash
    Pay in cash

Get fired.

Serve beignet
    Save the day
Saints win game
    Lake Pontchartrain
Step on stingray
    Piano Play

Get fired.

Slots played
    Pennies made
Crab sort
    Miss day in court
Louisiana storm
    Party in dorm

Get fired.

Nip moonshine
    Dress so fine
Play trombone
    Hang up the phone
Smoke some green
    French Quarter scene

Get fired.

Burn trash
    Earn some cash
Tourist Trap
    Suave rap
Eat boudin
    Steal his man

Get fired.

Clean hotel
    Suspicious smell
Shine shoes
    Card hand loose
Miss a bus
    Boss man fuss

Get fired.

Grandma said
    Jazz great dead
Second line
    Take your time
Mossy oak
    Rum and coke

Get fired.

Catch in the wind
    Wrong one offend
Kick wash pail
    Finger hangnail
Poisons brewed
    Subject lewd

Get fired.

Dog fleas
    Credit card fees
Holy Ghost
    Burn pot roast
Rescue folk
    Engine choke

Get fired.

Mardi Gras
    Abide the law
Gon get lit
    Done with this shit

Ash Wednesday
  Confess and pray
And
Still
Get
Fired.

PART 3

Earth

Window Pain. Digital photograph by Mel Michelle Lewis, 2023.

Elemental Essay: Earth

I am made of earth. What does earth elevate?

Center

I am born of the river confluence, the bay head, the gulf edge. I am in community with the bayou beings, the drawl kin.

Even'doe ise cityfolk
Ise that way
Ise married now
Ise done ran off

I am still, one'adem. Alice Walker describes this connection in "The Black Writer and the Southern Experience," writing, "What the black Southern writer inherits as a natural right is a sense of community. Something simple but surprisingly hard, especially these days, to come by."[1] Walker calls me into the sensory depth of home, the taste and smell of nature/culture. My mother gifted me a pink and purple copy of *In Search of Our Mothers' Gardens*, inherited; I've underlined the passage:

> In the cities it cannot be so clear to one that he is a creature
> of the earth, feeling the soil between the toes, smelling the dust
> thrown up by the rain, loving the earth so much that one longs
> to taste it and sometimes does.[2]

I've never told my mother what this means to me. But will.

The City City

As I read my favorite Black writers, and as a writer myself, I recognize, it is the earth that loves us to life. However, as Walker notes in the same text, "In the cities it cannot be so clear."[3] I live in Baltimore, a city where I have seen the enslaved and free Black community as ghosts who walk with us on the earth, in the night fog in the Fell's Point neighborhood. I owned a home deeded 1830, on a historic alley street housing Black Caulkers' Union workers, Frederick Douglass and Billie Holiday my neighbors, I know this city loves me.

I work in Washington, D.C., the capital city city, I advocate for healthy rivers, clean water, and environmental justice. Even here, in the capital city city, the river is not safe.

> The Anacostia
> Improved enough
> Over years
> For a Saturday, "splash"
> Announcement
> Due to Friday rains, "sewer"
> Overflows
> Clean rivers have been
> Postponed

In the city city, the air is viscous, the water is wretched, the earth buried beneath high tower tons and black top acrid. I am a creature who longs to taste my bayou home.

> The taste of the bayou murky mud
> The taste of the Gulf salty sea
> The taste of the air musty moss
> The taste of the house humid history

If I told you I grew up on a plantation, in a historic mansion, on the land, under the oaks, on the bayou, on the seashore?

If I told you my family enslaved and free Black, Native and Black, Creole and white, and Black and Black, own this land into the sea?

If I told you my childhood bedroom, overlooking the ocean, was bigger than any apartment I have ever lived in as an adult?

If I told you my grandmothers cooked soulful feasts in the kitchen, and we ate on china and paper plates, and drank from crystal goblets and red Solo cups, in the formal dining room?

If I told you much of my personality, affect, and parlance, come from Miss Flora. Filipina, a sista/mamma, five til' seventeen. Thank you beloved.

If I told you I have lived in, visited, and studied in the Philippines, Thailand, Singapore, France, Tunisia, England, Mexico?

If I told you my grandfather rode for miles around the property for hours each day on his lawnmower in the hot sun?

If I told you I can fish with a reel, shuck an oyster, cast a net, and catch a crab with a chicken leg on a piece of string?

If I told you I can make gumbo, fry catfish, make greens?

If I told you I can ride a horse and win a ribbon, and know the choreography to the Petipa ballets by heart?

If I told you people come from near and far to take pictures of the plantation home, unannounced, without permission, with me in my robe and slippers?

If I told you I am princess, only child of the Mardi Gras Queen and King, an heir of many family stories?

Maybe.
If I told you I am queer
Would you know, what the *maybe* is for?
For the spiral stair?
For the colossal columns?
For the harsh hurricanes?

For the oyster shell earth?
What would you say?
Would you believe it all?
It is true.

Laid in Earth

How this all came to be is an ongoing story, built upon the Ancestors, resting in their graves—or accompanying me, while I walk the earth. They rest, yes, but the Ancestors work for and with and through us. Enslaved and free Black and Native and Black and Creole and white and Black and Black and Black. They speak, conjure, protect, and intervene. When Jessye Norman or Leontyne Price sing "Dido's Lament" from the opera *Dido and Aeneas*, I hear the Ancestors in these words:

> When I am laid, am laid in earth, may my wrongs create
> No trouble, no trouble, in thy breast
> Remember me, remember me, but ah!
> Forget my fate.[4]

Their stories are mine, wrongs and troubles. I take this to mean many things beyond the context of the opera, when sung by Norman, earth daughter of Georgia, or Price, earth daughter of Mississippi. The Ancestors hope they have paved a better path for the next generation, and although I remember them, I need not be beholden to their lots in life. Indeed, I may also forget the fate of death. They implore me to remember them, for they are with me, and steer me through fate. My family's home and my own are shrines to the Ancestors, each wall and table covered with tintypes, Polaroids, digital photos, gelatin silver prints, and scans of images, framed watching, watching, singing, "remember me."

Cemetery

Ancestors work in mysterious ways. Our own lives are a continuation of theirs, cumulative, body, blood, and fate. If I told you my wife and I met for the first time, well into our careers and relationship-lives, at a conference, "Whose Beloved Community," then again in Baltimore, not knowing we had any community or familial connections, beyond our overlapping contemporary Black queer and scholarly pursuits?

If I told you we learned our families were both from Black Mobile, Alabama

If I told you our mammas had the same piano teacher?

If I told you a generation before, my uncle and my wife's cousin were roommates at Talladega College in the 1950s?

If I told you my cousin, and godmother, is married to my wife's cousin?

If I told you my father's babysitter was baseball legend Henry Aaron and my wife's classmate and college friend was Aaron's daughter, driving home together for college breaks.

If I told you the women in our families went to my wife's grandmother's salon to get their hair done?

If I told you my great-uncle and my wife's great-aunt have schools named for them a few miles apart?

If I told you my aunt and my wife's cousin and godmother were Dominican Sisters? The elder mentored the younger and the younger played musical interludes in her honor at her funeral. They are now both laid in earth, together, at the Sinsinawa Motherhouse? Together.

If I told you
Our Ancestors are
Laid in Earth
In the Black Catholic plot
In Oaklawn Memorial Cemetery

Facing each other
Our family ties
A narrow ribbon
Of earth
The path between them
Foot-to-foot
Seeing each other's souls
—what would you say?
Would you believe it all?
It is true.

Earthen Imprint

Earth grounds this section, thematically, through metaphor and turn of phrase. The first offering in this section, "Praise Song for the Road Home," celebrates the path that leads us to our past. The next selection, "What on Earth," employs elements of the travel narrative form. "What on Earth" uses multiple voices across generations to tell the story, an adaptation of a very true story told by my mother. "Erosion" explores my identity in the context of blood quantum, census documents, and the porous limits of non-enrolled Poarch Creek Indian Afrodescendant DNA.

Finally, the poem "Who Got the Body?" observes Black southern ritual burial and mourning. This poem is inspired by a passage from James Baldwin's *Giovanni's Room*: "The body in the mirror forces me to turn and face it. And I look at my body, which is under sentence of death. It is lean, hard, and cold, the incarnation of a mystery."[5] Under this sentence, I reflect upon "old death" and the generations who have moved away from the ancestral community's foodways, spiritual practices, and beliefs.

Earth Invocation for the Reader

May you dig deep
Till the land
Tool in hand
Forehead ashes
Prayers like dust
You shall return to
May you rest in earth
And rise
When your time comes

Praise Song for the Road Home

Road whose dirt is mixed with sand
Washed out and restored supreme way
Overcome not by sea battle nor wind howl
When home becomes a wave
Road with low bayou bridges built
In wood then paved then cemented in
Oh, curve of mystery and oak revelation
Path to immortal family portal
Road sacred east to west
Sun and moon follow direction
When time has passed in cycles
Remain and welcome the weary traveler
Road horseshoe crab process
To honor with ancient crackle and claw
Winding power invite first sight
The wave and joyous tear of Ma'muh
Road exalted by dolphins
The path mullet jump and worship
Divine route along the shore
Lead me to my ocean front door

What on Earth

I. Themgals

Cousin Monique and Cousin Saundra love to drive the shiny black Cadillac acrost the Bay. Papa 'laow them to drive it, go visit Aunt Sister, have them a picnic, when they home from college. Themgals roller set they hair the night before, even though they wear a silk scarf the whole way and back, so far as I know. Themgals slather themselves with a whole jar of Ponds Cold Cream and paint each other's toenails, even though erybody's skin is humid in summer and ain't nobody 'laowd to have they toes out nowhere. Themgals pick an outfit like they goin to a Mardi Gras Ball, even though they mostly just sittin in the car the whole way and back, so far as I know. Themgals line they eyes like cats, even though they wear sunglasses big as tea saucers the whole way and back, so far as I know. Mamma don't 'laow them to wear no loud lipstick nowhere. They blot red tube paint down to a precious rouge. Seem like it'll blow right off they lips soon as they hit the causeway, salt air and windows down. Cousin Monique and Cousin Saundra make like they Diana Ross and the Supremes getting ready for a world tour. Mamma don't 'laow them to make like they Tina Turner and the Ikettes.

Mamma say, "now y'all don't go actin grown," even though sophomore and junior year at Tuskegee shoal is nearly grown.

No back talk.

I'm bein nice and I'm bein good.

Mamma fix a lunch for Themgals and Aunt Sister. Biscuits with ham, pound cake, fried chicken, deviled eggs, mason jars of lemonade and bottles of root beer. Mamma fold up an old quilt to sit on, and a scratchy gray army wool blanket to spread on the earth beneath.

Mamma give Themgals an open envelope full of ladies' magazine clippings on how to fix yourself up nice, how to meet a gentleman, how to smell like flowers in the places that don't, how to cook easy recipes, and church bulletin prayer confetti.

To deliver Aunt Sister.

Papa give Themgals a sealed envelope full of cash money, so full it barely folds over to its own glue, and a long Dear Sister letter he take all week to write.

To deliver Aunt Sister.

Themgals hug and kiss everybody in the house and make like they sailin off to Paris like Josephine Baker, even though they comin back before dark, so far as I know.

I half expect them not to.

If'in only I could get away in a Cadillac acrost the Bay.

II. Go On'head

Just as I was thinkin on my Cadillac getaway, Mamma stand on the porch with a little suitcase, she take hold of me and half-lift me down the stairs. She hand Papa the little suitcase and me. Papa put the bag in the trunk with the picnic and shut it down like a fish bitin a hook it ain't never gonna shake.

"Go on'head and get in the car, Lil'mae, you finna stay with Aunt Sister till Mamma have the baby," say Papa.

Mamma kiss me on the forehead and hand me a peppermint. "Mamma loves you, Lil'mae, you be good now, you be nice. Go on'head." I look to see if she cryin like soap operas. She shut the screen door, I can't tell what face she makin from behind stiff spiderweb squares.

Themgals don't look at me.

"What on earth we finna do now," whisper Cousin Saundra. Cousin Monique fold her arms over her chest. They whispering something in they mind between'em but don't make a face.

Themgals start up the big shiny Cadillac ship and slowly push off. They ain't sorry I got to go stay with Aunt Sister.

I can see they jus' sorry they got to take me.

I can see they thought they was bout to have some fun in the black Cadillac.

I try to tell'em they can sing to the radio and gossip and drive too fast and wave at boys out the window like they on a Mardi Gras float.

I ain't gonna tell on nobody, but they act like they got stomach-aches and scowl and huff and puff and suck their teeth the whole way acrost the Bay.

III. She Gone

Mrs. Church bust out the house acrost the street when she see the black Cadillac. The screen door swing behind her and smack her wide bottom so hard she got to stumble down the steps. I try not to laugh.

"Shoot y'all, here come Mrs. Church," say Cousin Monique, rollin her eyes behind them sunglasses.

Monique purse her lips hard and start stopping the Cadillac ship, let it roll up in front of Aunt Sister's house. Mrs. Church stop and look at us, she stretch both of her arms above her head and wave, flop both hands up and down and call out with too much air escaping for her to finish anything she sayin.

"Hey there . . . whew lawd y'all came all this way . . . how y'all doin . . . she ain't here . . . whew you know she ain't here . . . she done ran off with That One again . . . you know the one . . . shoal nuf . . . she gone."

Cousin Monique and Cousin Saundra just look at each other. They whispering something in they mind between'em but don't make a face.

Mrs. Church make like we finna get out the car, but Cousin Monique and Cousin Saundra don't even let the window down to talk to Mrs. Church bout it. Monique put the Cadillac back in drive and slowly pull away with a half wave.

Mrs. Church who steady breathin out, "won't y'all come on and sit down . . . you wanna . . . whew did you bring . . . well who you got there . . . what y'all finna do?"

We launching the Cadillac again, so she just stand out in the street and wave with her heavy wet bosom handkerchief.

"What on earth we finna do now?" say Cousin Saundra.

Cousin Monique just drivin like we goin back home.

"We can't take Lil'mae back home!" Cousin Monique protest. "We sposed to leave her here." "Maybe we can ask Mrs. Church, if she don't mind, Lil'mae could . . ."

Cousin Saundra cut her short, "Na'ah, girl! Monique, we can't leave Lil'mae like that. She sposed to stay with Aunt Sister . . . maybe we can find where she at and take Lil'mae. Maybe we get to drive to Montgomery or Atlanta!"

"Umph, well," Cousin Monique think a long while, "umm hmm, let's go back and ask Mrs. Church if she know where to find Aunt Sister."

We turn the ship slowly, and dock back in front of Mrs. Church house. She start all over, she bust out the house, the screen door swing behind her and smack her on her wide bottom hard. I try, again, not to laugh. Mrs. Church gasp her greetings and wave again, "whew come on . . . who is that you got wit ya . . . don't you want to . . . what y'all done brought . . . whew she done ran off . . . with That One, you know . . . come on sit a while . . ."

I climb out of the Cadillac but my feet don't touch the ground. Mrs. Church scoop me up, breathin and holdin me tight and huggin and kissin me and dousing me with sweat. "Who is this precious baby . . . wha'chore name is . . . gimme some sugar baby . . . is this . . . shoal is ain't it, well you don't remember me . . . do ya . . . ain't you pretty . . . I remember when you was a lil baby . . . come on and sit down, y'all."

We climb up the steps and sit in the rocking chairs on the screened-in porch. "Don't y'all want some lunch? Lemme get you a slice of pie, what you want pretty baby? Y'all want some lemonade?"

I think Mrs. Church seem nice enough to stay with, don know why Themgals don't like that idea. I don't say nuthin bout wanting a pie. Yet.

"No mam, thank you," say Cousin Saundra, "we got to get on home, but we wanted to ask if you know where Aunt Sister is so we can . . ." Cousin Monique startle all of us. She sling her arm acrost Cousin Saundra's chest and push her in the rocking chair way back to the tips.

"Just—to visit with her, just to visit with her," say Cousin Monique in unconvincing suspicious dramatic perfect diction.

Cousin Saundra just trying not to tip over, she nodding, then cut me a look. I can hear her talkin in my mind not to say nuthin bout stayin with Aunt Sister or the money. I don't make a face.

I ain't said nothin this whole time I been sittin here in Mrs. Church's lap and ain't finna start now. I'm bein nice and good.

"Yes, I know where she at, if y'all wanna know." Mrs. Church squeeze me and hold me in her lap and press my head to her wet bosom handkerchief. She smell like wet earth. "Ummmmmmm hmmmmmmmmm . . . I shoal do." She say real slow. Themgals perk up and lean in like they bout to climb into Mrs. Church's lap too.

Mrs. Church breathe real heavy. She so excited to tell it, but want to make it last, like soap operas, so she go real slow. "Well . . . Your Aunt Sister done gone off to New Orleans . . . She done gone off with That One . . . You know, the one who come to call on her sometimes . . . the real pretty . . . nice one . . . was a nurse in the army . . ." Mrs. Church catch her breath, "real glamorous one, that brown one . . . the one with some money . . . the one that was in a movie . . . the one who can sing . . . That One, she got some real cash money . . . Real smart . . . The one used to come and stay sometimes . . . That One. Well, they done gone to New Orleans now."

I can hear Cousin Monique and Cousin Saundra talkin a little jealous of That One in they mind while she tellin it. They don't make a face.

"Did she say when she might be back?" Cousin Monique finally ask in a mournful voice.

"Naw chile, don't know that, but she closed up the house tight on the way out . . . asked me to look after the garden and I could have anything I want out it. She say not to worry bout the mail cause she had it held at the pos' office."

Cousin Monique and Cousin Saundra melt out of their rocking chairs, signal me to melt off of Mrs. Church's lap. "Well, thank you Mrs. Church, we shoal do appreciate you letting us know," Monique back to her regular people talkin.

"Well . . . ain't there something . . . you want to leave with me . . . from your Uncle Les . . . for your Aunt Sister? Something . . . cause I can give it . . . when she come . . . I can hold it for you . . . anything you need to . . ." Mrs. Church hopeful huffing and puffing. I wonder if she heard me talkin in my mind about the root beer in the car trunk and the money.

"No ma'am, thank you," Themgals say and herd me back into the car like a hen out the coop. We launch the ship and wave. Mrs. Church just hobble up the steps this time and don't look back.

IV. Present

Cousin Monique got us slowly drifting home in the Cadillac. I'm real hungry and got to go to use the bathroom. We pull off the road and I squat down behind the open car door while they get out lunch.

"We can eat while we drive," say Cousin Monique.

I know ain't no eating in Papa's Cadillac, but—I'm willing to get in trouble over it this time. Seem like we are in trouble anyhow, even though I'm being good and I'm bein nice.

As soon as I pull up my underpants, I know somebody watching me. I squeal and jump in the car. Themgals squeal and jump in the car too, without waiting to know what I'm squealing bout.

"What's the matter Lil'mae? You alright?" Cousin Saundra check me, leaning over the front seat and clawin at me with her hands. "Come on, girl, let's go!" she squeal at Monique.

The trunk is still open, and the key is in the lock, so somebody got to get out. I try to tell'em he watching us, he in the ditch, comin toward us, but they busy trying to think how they gonna get out and close the trunk and jump back in the car.

Just then, I see him!

He got a blue neck and little pea head and black and white on the body and long legs and look like a turkey that got on a lady's nightgown. He hop up out of the ditch and skip flap over to the Cadillac. Themgals scream. He scream. He got a louder scream than the two of them together.

"Is that . . ." say Cousin Sandra when she open her eyes and look.

"A peacock!" say Cousin Monique when she peek.

I just look out my window down at the long neck and little floppy crown he got on his little blue pea head. He real close and I can see he got pretty eyes and a pointy beak. I can tell Themgals almost bout to cuss out loud but they sayin it in they mind to each other, don't make a face.

Peacock! He lookin at himself in the side of the shiny black Cadillac, he must like what he lookin at, he screamin and make his whole lady's nightgown stand up and shimmy. He peck at the door.

"What on earth we finna do now?" say Cousin Saundra.

"Well we can't drive with the trunk open, and we can't let this thing peck a hole in the door, Uncle Lou is gonna kill us," say Cousin Monique. "The keys are in the the trunk so I can't start the car." They both turn to me in the back seat.

"Lil'mae, get out the car on the other side from the peacock and get the keys out the trunk and bring em here." I slide acrost the seat and get out, I sneak around to the back of the car. I can't reach the trunk or the keys to get em out. I peek around at Peacock, he just lookin at himself in the mirror of the shiny black door. He peckin, like he knocking on it to get in. I sneak around and get back in the car. Themgals lookin for me to hand them the keys, I try to tell'em I can't reach nuthin like they said. I try to tell'em he ain't so bad as I thought. He just lookin pretty at himself in the car door, maybe he just knockin to get in like folks with good manners.

Cousin Monique pursin her lips and get out the car slowly to close the trunk and get the keys, tiptoe. Cousin Saundra scoot over in the driver's seat to watch what Cousin Monique doin.

"What on earth is a peacock doing on the side of the road in the middle of nowhere?" she yell.

Cousin Monique yell back, "Ain't no wild peacocks in Alabama!" She make it back to the car, slam the door shut, start the engine.

I pull the door lever, see if I can kiss Peacock goodbye on his little pea head and tell him "Go on'head" and pat his soft blue neck. The whole car door swing open and I fall out the car and roll way down in the ditch. Themgals start screaming all over again. Peacock start screaming all over again. I claw up the muddy ditch and scramble back into my seat.

Soon as I get in, Peacock hop and skip flap into the back of the car with me. He sit on me with his tail across the seat like a stiff quilt. Sittin there in my lap, I see he got a round fat tummy and seem about the same size as I am but he ain't too heavy. He just sit in my lap lookin like he ready for Cousin Monique to take him where he want to go.

Themgals jump out and run round the car in circles screaming and hollering and opening and closing the doors and tellin me to get out of the car. But I got Peacock sittin on me and can't get up. He being nice, he being good. I'm being nice and good too.

Afterwhile, Themgals start laughing and peeking in the window instead of screaming.

There is a peacock in the Cadillac.

"What on earth we finna do now?" say Cousin Saundra.

Cousin Monique think a long while, "umm hmm." She say, "Ok, how bout we gonna take him home. Uncle Lou gonna like this peacock, don't nobody got one. You know he like to show off. This is even better than a Cadillac!"

"Umph," Cousin Saundra clap her hands. Might not be in such big trouble over Lil'mae coming back with us if we bring a present too," she say. "Nobody believe us tellin it unless we had it to show em."

Don't nobody want Peacock flappin and hopping around in the Cadillac on the way home, so Cousin Monique got the picnic quilt out the trunk. "Lil'mae, see if he will let you put this on him." I put the picnic quilt over the peacock then pull it around under his fluffy front and tuck the rest in my lap. He just nest into me like a hen with his tail across the seat and didn't mind one bit.

"Lil'mae, you gonna hold on to him and don't let him move around while we drivin, you hear me?" He ain't said nothin this whole time he been sittin here in my lap and ain't finna start now. We bein nice and good.

I hope Papa keep him.

I hope Papa keep me too.

Erosion

Black scholars scold

Every
Black family claims
Grandma
[Was] a
Cherokee princess

Black scholars told

Every
Long braid legend was
[Only] a
Plantation harvest

The Poarch Creek Indian Tribal Roll[6] is currently closed at this time.

Mother, we are Sehoy's Wind Clan children
Although
We do not appear
On the roll

I can
[Only] complete
An incomplete application for membership

I can
Complete a Pedigree Chart
All supporting evidence [DNA test, birth certificates, etc.]
Is
[Also] Black Earth

I have not been eldered
And so, it is hard
To know how
[Not] to be a
Pretendian
The only thing
I am eligible for

I say
I am Black
Unless there is
Enough time for
A long wind
An un/earth

Non-enrolled Poarch Creek Indian Afrodescendant

In some cases
I say
So

In some cases
Census says
The same person
Is Indian
I
Is White
W
Is Black

B
Is Colored
C
Is Mulatto
M
Depending
How the taker
Took them

There were
Marriages
Households
Affairs
Unmarried lovers
Two-timers
Travels
Rendezvous
Births

But no birth certificates
But no adoption papers

Mother, you swore an affidavit
[In the 1980s]
So that Grandmother could receive
A birth certificate
[She wanted to travel]
It said
She was born
[Around 1911]
Nothing more to document

There were
Knowings
Knowing blood parents

Knowing blood grandparents
Knowing blood great-grandparents
Knowing blood and kin

I can not be unmade

Now DNA
Now Ancestry.com matches
Now common ancestors
Now blood quantum
But not enough
[Now]

I can enumerate
Mother can enumerate
Moniac
Colbert
Richardson
Mississippian

I was always going
Going to the reservation
Going to the pow wows
Going to the family tree
Going to the earthen dance

As a child, I planned to be
A princess
Before I knew
I was not eligible
I dressed and danced
[Outside]
The circle
Without knowing
I was non-enrolled

I belonged to
Something partial
I belonged to
Someone whole
A Grandmother Moniac

I learned
My few Muskogee words
From the mouth of
A Princess

Hello Hensci
Thank you Mvto

Who Got the Body?

I. LAST RITES
Breath released
For the last time
From this body

Bedside Father
Son
Holy ghosts
Anoint
Make the sign of the cross

II. DEATH
Into your hands I commend my spirit
For it is to be commended
For all it has accomplished
Ashes to ashes
Dust to dust

Make me an altar
Serve me
For I have served

Make arrangements

When they ask
Who got the body?

Tell'em Jenkins Funeral Home
Will do me

III. VISITATION
Gather together
At the house

He in a better place
He lived a full life
I'm sorry for your loss

Bring soulful dishes

The health-conscious Olympic New York Son
The doctor Los Angeles Daughter
The foodie Chicago Grandchild
The political Washington, D.C., Grandchild
The vegetarian Seattle Nephew
The gluten-free San Francisco Niece
The vegan art school Great-grandchildren
Will not eat

Eat

Tell a story
Remember that time when I _____.
Did you ever know that I _____.
Cry
He gone

Fight
The survivors in the obituary

The arrangements
The casket
The cost
The time
The order of service
The program
The survivors in the obituary
Fight

Listen to a story
You never thought that I _____.
You can't recall when I _____.
Cry
He gone

He in a better place

Do an impression of me
Laugh
He gone

Fight
The survivors in the obituary
Money
Property
Will
Furniture
That old thing
Favorites
The survivors in the obituary
Fight

Say that thing, I always used to say
Laugh
He gone

Begin to get used to saying
Used to

IV. WAKE
Dress yourself in black
The small children in white

Save your funeral suit
For tomorrow

Open casket
Look
At me
Resting

Done up
Bronze Liberace
Pretty
Like the mortician
Mr. Framboise Jenkins
My last intimate

He look real good
They say
They shoal did a good job on the body
He look jus'like himself
They say

Agreed

Folk cry out (but not the Catholics)
Why Jesus!
Folk cry out (but not the Catholics)
Lawd why!

I was nearly ninety-nine

Handkerchiefs
Hugs
Hemmin'and hawin

A packed parking lot
Smokers with
Sips of something
On cell phones
Executive relatives in
Rented Escalades
On cell phones
Cousins who've never met
Half flirting
On cell phones

Close me in
Lower the lid
Let me be

V. FUNERAL
Now wear
Your best black suit

The one you wear
To speak at conferences
To do TV interviews
To make corporate deals
To bury the dead

The one they wear
From Walmart
The one they wear

From Salvation Army
The one they wear
Auntie take in or out, sew from a pattern
To bury the dead

Funeral Mass
Father
Son
Holy ghosts
Anoint
Make the sign of the cross

Sing the songs
Genuflect (not the Protestants)
Dab your tears
Take communion (not the Protestants)

Wheel me out
Carry me down
Hoist me into
The carriage
The Excelsior Band awaits

VI. PROCESSION
Ten pieces of brass
Herald my departure
From this earth

Three trumpets
Three saxophones
One trombone
One tuba
One bass drum
One snare drum

Moving slowly to the gravesite
As in life
One step at a time
On the beat

The sun and humidity
Tax the living
Sweat
Heave
Perspire
Huff

Swelter

Many refuse
The jazz funeral procession
Delicate disposition
Nice shoes
Comfortable cars and air condition
Meet me at my grave
Come ready for the earth to take me

VII. BURIAL
Now I lay me down to sleep
Mr. Framboise Jenkins
Gestures
White gloves
Theatrical
Sit and watch

Receive
My folded flag
Fought for
You

Place your flowers on my coffin
Each an ancestral offering

Turn to leave me
With a last tear
Under this tree
Undertakers
Will dirty themselves to
Inter me

Who got the body?

Earth

VIII. REPAST
Serve soulful dishes

The health-conscious Olympic New York Son
The doctor Los Angeles Daughter
The foodie Chicago Grandchild
The political Washington, D.C., Grandchild
The vegetarian Seattle Nephew
The gluten-free San Francisco Niece
The vegan art school Great-grandchildren
Will not eat

Eat

Say your goodbyes

Make your plane
Make your train
Make your eighteen-hour drive
Be sure to arrive

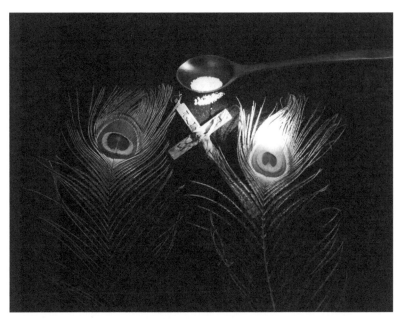

Salt Sanctuary. Digital photograph by Mel Michelle Lewis, 2023.

PART 4

Mineral

Slave schedule 2, City of Mobile, Alabama, 1850. National Archives.

Elemental Essay: Mineral

I am mineral made. What does mineral mine?

Ancestry
Blood relatives, kin, and my people, we are made of the same
    minerals, a connection biochemical. These connections are
    told through oral traditions, the inscriptions in the family
    Bible, and now, on Ancestry.com DNA!
You the spit'in image of
You shoal favor
No question who ya'daddy is
Ya'mamma family got that good Indian hair
Forehead, nose, chin, cheekbone
Lazy eye see who you ise

Ancestors are mineral, material and illusion. In *The Salt Eaters*,
Toni Cade Bambara names the mineral seeing "eye of the heart"
and its truth pursuit.

Solids, liquids, molecules, ethers, electrical charges. The eyes
and habits of illusion. Retinal images, bogus images, traveling
the brain. The pupils trying to tell the truth to the inner eye.
The eye of the heart. The eye of the head. The eye of the mind.
All seeing differently.[1]

I apply this to Ancestors; some belong to the heart and fleshy parts
deep in the mineral mines of my marrow histories. Others belong

to the head; they are remembered, dreamed. In the census, some folks are blood mineral, numbered "1" enslaved body, with "age, sex, and color" on a "slave schedule." Other folks are stones worn down from seventeen generations back in the Netherlands. In "On the Pulse of Morning," Maya Angelou writes of the mineral shoulders we stand on:

> The Rock cries out to us today,
> You may stand upon me,
> But do not hide your face.[2]

We cannot hide our faces. These are the documented lines to my Ancestors, written in the thin-skinned grotto under my eye.

We trace the chemical blood and structured bone; we plot the mineral properties, the bodies of water, of solid rock. I come from the in-between. Dehumanized and destroyed, royal and resplendent, the minerals of those who landed, and those who took flight, all mark me, legitimized and let be.

How does mineral work itself free?

Slave Schedule

NAMES OF SLAVE OWNERS.
Number of slaves.
Age.
Sex.
Color.
Fugitive from the state.

These are among the horizontal categories on the 1850 and 1860 census "slave schedules." My wife, librarian and archivist Kerrie Cotten Williams, and I have examined my preoccupation with the "number of slaves" category. In most documents, a "1" is marked for each of the enslaved, hash marks down the page. Mineral bodies but nameless. Individual. Human. Each "1" reads as an "I" in iron gall ink, iron sulfate, and tannic acid. My mineralogy. Solid compounds.

I (am) 30 M B
I (am) 16 F B

Why was the "slave schedule" census document designed with a redundant column, number of slaves, one slave per slave? "1" enslaved-human-body-property per age, sex, color. Individual. One mineral being each. In this peculiar metaphysical mathematics, we were miscounted. "How many slaves," one "I (am)" each, no more, no less. Or so they wrote, but we are multiple.

Cumulative Minerals

They could not have written a number big enough to say how many "1" is.

How do we as writers, artists, teachers, hear then amplify the voice to the "I (am)"; indeed it is our voice, for we are cumulative mineral. Nothing that I have ever said or will ever say has been said without them. Although cross-referencing a number of other records can help to fill in the "1" or "I (am)" penned in curling-iron cursive; indeed, the ink black is written on our faces.

Bound in Wedlock

Kinship is beyond what is written in ink. Yet ink can tell us about some of our minerals. In *Bound in Wedlock: Slave and Free Black Marriage in the Nineteenth Century*, Tera W. Hunter points out that, "As chattel, slaves were objects *not* subjects. Marriage for them was not an inviolable union between two people but an institution defined and controlled by the superior relationship of master to slave."[3] In many cases, this means we have no record of these relationships between "I (am)" and "I (am)," an "us," 1+1 = 2. However, some of my free Black Ancestors have documented names, records, and inviolable unions. There are also records of those caught between liquid and solid.

My ancestral auntie Sallie Critty was arrested and brought to trial in 1860 for "cohabitating with a slave." As a free mulatto woman and landowner, it was illegal for enslaved persons to live in her household. Sallie pled not guilty and was fined one copper penny, according to court records. We do not know who the "I (am)" in Sallie's home was, or what relationship they had, but I imagine it was magnetic; they could not be kept from each other. Igneous rock, magnetite.

My wife and I are bound in wedlock; with our roots in Alabama's Mobile communities, we reclaim the inviolable for our Ancestors and for ourselves. Just as laws and perspectives on marriage equality shifted over time for our Ancestors— enslaved and free, Black, white, Creole, and native—marriage laws have changed for us as well. As Catherine E. McKinley writes in the introduction to *Afrekete: An Anthology of Black Lesbian Writing*, "We are two girls looking for our stories."[4] And so, we preserve, research, write, and live them. Our stories, for all of us. As Audre Lorde describes this living in *Zami: A New Spelling of My Name*:

> Zami. A Carriacou name for women who work together as friends and lovers. We carry our traditions with us. Buying boxes of Red Cross Salt and a fresh corn straw broom . . . new living the old in a new way. Recreating in words the women who helped give me substance.[5]

We make home and welcome all of our Ancestors in.

Mineral Alchemy

Salt is biblical and bodily, sacred and profane. The mineral element, through salt, iron, and calcium, serves to ground this section, in the past and in the present—in the body and in the blood. Colossians 4:6 instructs:

> Let your speech always be gracious, seasoned with salt, so that you may know how you ought to answer each person.

Audre Lorde discloses:

> and wherever I touch you
> I lick cold from my fingers
> taste rage
> like salt from the lips of a woman
> who has killed too often to forget
> and carries each death in her eyes[6]

In this section, readers may experience a mineral opacity, the licking of dense rocks, the melting salt on the tongue. The first piece, "Salt," presents a past that can still be seen and felt. Set in nineteenth-century Mobile, "Salt" explores kinship, queerness, and character through a sensory lens and draws from the history of the red-light district and Mobile's other "flesh trade."[7]
Langston Hughes and Richard Wright propose:

> I want to tramp in the red mud, Lawd, and
> Feel the red clay round my toes.
> I want to wade in that red mud,
> Feel that red clay suckin' at my toes.[8]

Savory humid mineral soil grounds the next piece. "Red Clay Recipe" is a celebration of earthen sensuality, queer discovery, and Black community cultural contexts, connecting the elemental to the corporeal.

This recipe poem is influenced by Michael Twitty and his influential cookbook, memoir, and historical study, *The Cooking Gene:*

A Journey through African American Culinary History in the Old South.[9] This poem sculpts sexuality from youthful awakenings to corporeal connections.

Gwendolyn Brooks depicts the magnetic mundane between lovers as they begin their daily routine:

> In a package of minutes there is this We.
> How beautiful.
> Merry foreigners in our morning,
> we laugh, we touch each other,
> are responsible props and posts.[10]

"Indian Shell Mound Park" examines partnership and place. How does Black queer love root down, in a place so overtaken by the sea, and nature? The final poem, "Oyster Shuck," invites the reader to grapple with the mineral corporeality and vulnerability of Black queer experience.

Mineral Invocation for the Reader

> May you taste clay
> On your tongue and tell the truth
> Your Ancestors are
> The salt
> Inside
> May you lift the heavy stones
> On the grave
> And give free

Oyster Honey. Digital photograph by Mel Michelle Lewis, 2023.

Salt

Ant' Rosetta throw spilled salt over her left shoulder. She don (really) believe in the devil, the way she sposedto, but she believe in salt. Ant' Rosetta wear a long black dress with a lacy high neck, cinched by a sandy velvet sash with a brooch in the middle, even in August. She got black boots, black lace gloves, a high bun stabbed into place by a combination of jeweled hat pins. She got a fine black lace parasol, with frayed edges and a few strands of moss that got so wove in it ain't really worth pickin'em out. She got a stiff black veil over her forehead; it crinkles just enough to keep out of her eyes. Ant' Rosetta don (really) believe in dyin, the way she sposedto, but she believe in mourning. I ast her why she don wear nuthin but black. She say, "Always somebody dead or bout to die, chile."

Ant' Rosetta live ready.

Ant' Rosetta live alone.

In the Magnolia.

She don (really) believe in marriage and children, the way she sposedto, but—she believe in family. Un'cle Cletus and Daddy Rufus used to stay there too. They don (really) mind how the Magnolia smell like acifidity and candle smoke and hot honey-suckles and roux and boiled peanuts and salt air and dusty feathers and oyster liquor and bourbon and Poisson the wet dog and burnt praline sugar. But lawd know Un'cle Cletus done went and married Miss Faint Gautier of Pascagoula and Daddy Rufus done went and married Miss Helena Bellefontaine of Biloxi. The fine ladies might'a thought they was finna live like royalty at the Magnolia, but they ain't finna live up in the house with Ant' Rosetta, no matter how fine the livin. They don't even let they chilren visit, but they let us outside-chilren alone.

Ant' Rosetta invite all'us to come and stay. Un'cle Cletus and Daddy Rufus got plenty outside chilren to keep house and visit and tend the garden and fish the bayou and climb the oak trees. Un'cle Cletus and Daddy Rufus come round with outside chilren after sunrise and gather em'up and send em'home before sunset. I like to stay over. I ain't too fond of livin with Miss Helena Bellefontaine of Biloxi and them 'gitimate chilren. They don (really) believe in outside chilren like me, they ain't sposedto . . . They believe in blood. They all call me Lock. Miss Helena Bellefontaine of Biloxi been carrin'on bout "out of wedlock" so much, it got the little chilren thinkin. Once they could talk enough to call me out my name, they did. But I don really mind. "Lock" sounds just bout like what I am.

Ant' Rosetta the only one who don (really) mind what I am. Ise the only one who don (really) mind what she is neither. Folks only fraid of Ant' Rosetta cause they fraid of dying. The two of us don (really) need much from the livin anyhow. Ant' Rosetta ain't my mamma, but she do right by me just like she do right by the dying and the dead and the ghosts and the spirits and the saints and the souls. She do carry me to see my mamma in Mobile sometimes, when there's a funeral happening. Ant' Rosetta don't miss no big-time funerals.

Ant' Rosetta let me off at St. Michael and Warren Streets, she let me walk the rest of the way, even though I (really) ain't sposedto.

My mamma live in Doves House with Madame Leontine, who got a (real) name, like Mary Jones or Sarah Brown. Doves House got beautiful women and piano music and curling smoke and fine liquor and nice rugs and sweet snacks and heavy drapes and soft furniture and fine china. Don't nobody use no (real) name up in there. Madame Leontine open the big wooden door and pull me into her bosom. She hold me there till the door is bolted back. They ain't officially open till everybody done had their "beauty rest" and a chance to gossip and drink coffee and eat pastries and take a swig of liquor or a curl of smoke. Madame Leontine say, "let sleeping dogs lie." She (really) ain't talkin bout my mamma. Madame Leontine give me a cold glass of lemonade with a splash or two of bourbon and a cube of sugar and a swirl of honey. She give me a plate of pastries and wrap me in a fancy shawl, she tell me sit on the méridienne and pile me in with fluffy pillows that smell like cologne and iron and ships and sweat and tobacco and seagrass and bourbon lemonade.

Ant' Rosetta ain't comin back till after the repast, and mamma ain't hardly awake yet. I settle in to my nest. Miss María Camila, who joined the Doves last year and ain't ran off with no seaman or businessman or real man yet, finish her piano playing and brush crumbs and sticky candy off the keys with her silver silk robe. She don't got nothin else on and that's just fine fa me. Miss María Camila ain't much older than me, she dainty and round in the places I'm stout and plain. She seem like she from far away somewhere like New Orleans. Miss María Camila come to curl up on the méridienne with me. She talk like she still got pastries and candies in her mouth; I don't understand too much of what she say and I can tell she don't catch most of what I say, so we don't say too much, other than "hello" and "thank you" a few too many times. She pull her legs up to her chest and fold up next to me, she stick her feet under the back of my thighs and just smile and hold on to my forearm like a boat oar. She kiss me on the cheek and plait and unplait my braid, she kiss me where my smile curls and where my chin juts.

Mamma wake me up patting me on the head like Poisson the wet dog. "Musta been a good nap," mamma say. Miss María Camila dressed in bloomers and a corset and back playin piano with a glass of wine and a bowl of candy.

Ant' Rosetta say Mamma got a life.

Ant' Rosetta say Mamma love me.

But she live free at Doves House wit Miss Leontine. Mamma done went-and-got-a-baby with Daddy Rufus, that can happen sometimes. I was her "pretty lil'baby," but Mamma (real) fine and don't got no business raisin no chilren. She got a life. I understand. Ain't nuthin more to say bout it. Mamma don (really) know nuthin bout chilren. She send me a letter about seamen and some paper dolls to dress at Christmas and fa my birthday. She don (really) know young chilren ain't sposedto know some things bout seamen. She don (really) know chilren get too grown to like paper dolls. I rather play boat oars with Miss María Camila.

Mamma ain't like nobody's mamma. She got on a fancy gown the color of rusted iron and a whole lot'a perfume and her hair in a long braid over her shoulder. She got on a whole jewelry shop too. Mamma keep her skin soft and white, but—ain't (really) white. I favor Daddy Rufus, we turn metallic in the sun, and that's just fine fa me.

Ant' Rosetta say my mamma work late and sleep till noon. Ant' Rosetta don (really) say what she do, but I know. Mamma got a life. She serve bourbon lemonade with a cube of sugar and play boat oars with seamen. Ant' Rosetta arrange wit Miss Leontine when I'ma come call on them during a funeral. Mamma mostly don't know what day it is or if I'm comin till I'm there, but she love me and glad to see me and pat me on the head like Poisson the wet dog when she wake up.

It ain't early enough for Mamma to still be dressed up from last night and it ain't late enough to be dressed up like that to go nowhere yet. Mamma got a life. She pat me on the head some more and ask me if I want some coffee. I figure Miss Leontine done put an extra spoon of bourbon in my lemonade, so I might (really) be in need of a cup of coffee. Mamma hold her gown out and lower herself into a chair like a ceremonial ship launching. She pour coffee into dainty fine porcelain cups like a queen at court. She wave her hands guiding the coffee smell to her nose. Mamma take her coffee with salt. She sprinkle salt into the cup and stir slowly with a silver spoon.

Seamen say, salt get rid of the bitterness.

Red Clay Recipe

"Chile, git dat thumb out cho' mouth!"
Asberry suck his thumb

Prep time: done snuck off—till "Asberry, git your behind in heah and set this dinner table!"

Servings: As much as you want, YOU made it!

Ingredients

One suspenseful Friday soap
    opera
Three gossip phone calls to
    Ma'muh
Layers of Edna's romance novels in
    a cookie tin

Piping hot sun
Paste of c o o l r e d c l a y from
    under the back porch
Two thumbs

Steal away.

Preparation

Step 1
Bake innocently on the back stairs in sight of Ma'muh for
    three minutes until forgotten
Once the brow begins to sweat, slowly fold onto the ground
Roll under the porch

Step 2
Break open the cookie tin, select a steamy romance novel
Peel the humid pages apart carefully
Spread the book-body out on the c o o l r e d c l a y
Turn the pages
Press chest, stomach, hips, and thighs into the earth
Repeat until tender
Turn the body and allow the spine to sink into c o o l r e d c l a y
Let s t e a m

Step 3
Spread arms and legs to full length
Twist wrist and allow fingers to grasp c o o l r e d c l a y
Mold into desired shape
Release molded clay
Do not remove paste of c o o l r e d c l a y from hands

Step 4
Insert thumb into mouth
Repeat with remaining thumb
"Asberry, chile come set this dinner table!"

After Dinner
Dessert

"Hey man, you keep Morehouse out the end zone for this Home-
coming game, ya heard!"
Asberry put a hurtin on Morehouse last year
Tuskegee Golden Tigers—21, Morehouse Maroon Tigers—0

Prep time: Homecoming Weekend

Servings: As much as you want, YOU made it!

Ingredients

One fine Tuskegee Institute drum
   major uniform
One handsome Tuskegee Institute
   drum major (Framboise
   Jenkins, if available)

Two large prepared HBCU
   marching bands
Two medium-keen football teams
Paste of c o o l r e d c l a y from
   the gridiron
Rain

Preparation

Step 1
Add two medium keen football teams to the first half
Begin mincing cool wet red clay under cleats
Roll bodies through the clay, cover each player thoroughly

Step 2
Once half of the game has been played, begin halftime show
Spread luscious gyrations, marching, and musical fanfare evenly
   across the gridiron
Allow Framboise Jenkins to gyrate independently
Slowly add rain

Step 3
Continue the second half of the game
Baste Asberry generously in cool wet red clay paste
Crush the Morehouse Maroon Tigers

Step 4
End football game
Mill around
Soak Asberry in accolades
Introduce new ingredients [Framboise Jenkins, in drum major
   uniform]

Let both marinate in "Hey man . . ."
Allow time for ingredients to bind
Bring to a boil
Allow Framboise Jenkins to
Peel Asberry from admirers

Steal away.

Taste c o o l r e d c l a y
Massage into skin
Let s t e a m

Indian Shell Mound Park

Ollie and LaWanda live on Dauphin Island
Not in the ritzy raised creole cottages of
Confederate Pass or Colony Cove
LaWanda say
"Like hell! I ain't livin in nobody's 'confederate colony,' umph,
    umph, umph!"

Ollie and LaWanda live in a little house
Near Point Isabel
The estuary and little landing strip
On Ollie's grandmother's plot of land
The only Black-owned land on the island
So far as anybody can say

Ollie and LaWanda met at University of Alabama
"Roll Tide!"
In the library's graduate studies reading room
Ollie wrote a marine science master's thesis
On ocean acidification and oyster shell thinning
LaWanda wrote a women's studies Master's thesis
On Johnnie Carr and the often-ignored Black women
Organizers of the Montgomery Bus Boycott

Ollie and LaWanda don't look nuthin alike
But folks in the Ship & Shore Supply general store be askin

"A—A—A' y'all sisters?"

Affectionate Brown be like that
Got to be a good reason why
Got to be the same iron
Blood relatives
Who Black would choose and be chose back
Like that
That way

Most folks just curious

Ollie visit Montgomery with LaWanda now'nthen
Folks be askin
"A—A—A' y'all related?"
Ollie tell'em "Yep, that's my girl, ya heard"
LaWanda tell'em "Ummhmmm, that there's my heart"
Ollie and LaWanda don't hold hands in public
But they sleep holding hands every night

Ollie and LaWanda have a routine
Making messes and tidying up
Ollie tracks sand
All through the house
LaWanda quick to draw the Dustbuster
"Ollie! I know you love the beach but, Honey, you know you ain't
    got to have it inside the house too!"
LaWanda light incense
Play Jill Scott
Get her mind right
Ollie just laugh, "Bae I know, I know, I know . . ."
Go sit outside for a spell
LaWanda spread books and papers and notepads
All through the house

Ollie turn Muddy Waters up real loud
Read the titles and abstracts of each paper
Make piles with Post-it note labels and draw up a map
Indicating where LaWanda's thoughts were found, and where
    they got put up
Ollie don't tend to mention the recycled crumpled pieces of paper
LaWanda don't tend to ask

Ollie and LaWanda have a practice
Of letting some things alone
Ollie leave gadgets and disassembled gizmos
On countertops and tables
LaWanda let Ollie alone bout that
LaWanda leave pens and highlighters bleeding polka dots
On clothes and furniture
Ollie let LaWanda alone bout that

Ollie and LaWanda walk or ride bikes around the island
No emissions and no need for a car
Ollie got a Schwinn beach cruiser
Seven speed
LaWanda got a Barbella adult tricycle
With a wide seat and a basket on the back
LaWanda speed

Ollie and LaWanda got their own style
They call it "Afrofuturist Bass Pro"
Ollie got convertible cargo pants, unzip the knees
Ollie got a collection of pant legs that won't zip back on to the
    shorts
Ollie got "Black women in STEM" conference T-shirts
Ollie got mineral-infused moisture-wicking fabric sport marina
    shirts
LaWanda got Afrocentric wrap and maxi dresses full of island
    breeze

LaWanda got mudcloth and kente and linen
LaWanda got sustainable wood and handmade oyster shell jewelry
LaWanda got vegan Teva Manatee Sandals
Ollie and LaWanda ain't vegan

Ollie and LaWanda like to try recipes from Black women's
   cookbooks
Edna Lewis
Leah Chase
Ollie got a fangirl chef crush on Toni Tipton-Martin
LaWanda got a fangirl chef crush on Mashama Bailey
Both got a fangirl chef crush on Nina Compton
Ollie make a mean gumbo and grill surf and turf on the weekends
LaWanda bake pound cake, bread pudding, key lime pie, and
   keep pralines in
Abundance

Ollie and LaWanda take their work seriously
Listen and learn from each other
Ollie got a researcher job
At Dauphin Island Sea Lab
LaWanda got a researcher job
At Dora Franklin Finley African American Heritage Trail

Ollie and LaWanda have a standing date on Fridays
To discuss the close of the workweek, and transition
Into weekend freedom
Ride bikes to Indian Shell Mound Park
Sit on the bench under the oak tree

Ollie and LaWanda unpack
A mason jar of cold cubed watermelon and
Two sets of bamboo chopsticks
Being Black and
Eating watermelon in public
Breaking the rules, a little

Ollie say, "damn girl, you know ..."
LaWanda say, "I shoal do"
They just sit eatin and lookin and laughin at each other
Till it's time to get down to business

Ollie and LaWanda explain
Transformative work

Ollie on a project
Writing a curriculum on marine calcifiers
Explaining to Black high school students from systemically
     under-resourced schools
How calcium carbonate shells and skeletons are formed
LaWanda on a project
Including Black women's narratives and
Adding a gender analysis
To the heritage tour scripts

Ollie and LaWanda visit the shell mounds
To lay down burdens
The Mississippian Ancestors offer whispers
Moss breeze
A ritual of release

LaWanda got incense cones and a lighter
LaWanda got oils and stones and sage and sprigs of rue
Ollie got a notepad and pen and old handkerchief
Ollie got a passed-down jeweled hatpin
They make ceremony

Offerings
To the shell middens
A mass grave for
What needs shucking

Oyster Shuck

Oysters are opposites of themselves
Hard shell
Soft body
Like people

Oysters could swim the whole ocean
But sleep together
In their anchored pool
A fatal flaw

Oysters are collected and cleaned
Outside muck
After bathing the whole ocean
Inside fresh

Oysters close tight
Two sides
Have a vulnerable hinge
Like people

Oysters receive
Gentle violent
Blade twist
Release promise

Oysters go down
In their liquor

PART 5

Nature

Half Full. Digital photograph by Mel Michelle Lewis, 2023.

Elemental Essay: Nature

Nature is the wild way. What does nature impart?

Double Entendre
The nature of writing nature.
It is my nature to be multiple in my meaning.
The nature of writing nature.
It is nature that is many in its manner.

I am becoming a "nature writer." Yes, I am trained to write about the "nature" of power and oppression, race, class, gender, sexuality, the social "nature" of our condition. In "Simone de Beauvoir and *The Second Sex*," Lorraine Hansberry, another nature writer, explores the nature of oppression:

A status not freely chosen or entered into by an individual or a group is necessarily one of oppression and the oppressed are by their nature (i.e., oppressed) forever in ferment and agitation against their condition and what they understand to be their oppressors.[1]

I write about the "nature" of social ferment, microorganismpeople systemically breaking down. I am learning to also write about the nurturing power of "nature." Nature is a healer. Malidoma Patrice Somé describes this power to heal the human body, mind, and spirit in *Of Water and the Spirit*:

I could even hear nature, its relentless vibration of love and its slow movements. Its nurturing power fed me through my nose and my pores, sustaining my vital senses. I was aware that nature also fed itself in a way that I was not able to understand, but I knew it was not the kind of meal I could consume. I had friends in the trees and in the grass.[2]

Nature is a healer and a teacher. I am becoming both.

I am also becoming a "southern writer." As a scholar seeking high-impact journal and anthology placements in my field, my focus was on research and synthesis. This has not disappeared from my writing style, but I rely much more on memory, imagination, experience, and sensation, with a strong commitment to the politics of citation. This citation practice is no longer about illustrating my knowledge of the field and crediting ideas and discourses, but rather, it is a Womanist practice, illustrating the nature of love and lineage. In the words of Alice Walker, "*Loves the folk, Loves herself. Regardless.*"[3]

As an undergraduate student in women's studies, I struggled to understand a Womanist lesson taught by my white professor, asserting that nothing is "natural or normal" about race, class, gender, sexuality, or any other marker of identity or experience. Rather, as I understood the lesson at the time, everything oppressive about racial identity is "socially constructed." What we call "identity" itself is a construct. I was not sure about this; I believed my markers of identity to be my "nature." I explored further; a few degrees later, I took this lesson and made distinctions for my own students. Our "nature" is not just an assemblage of social constructions, but an illumination of the lived material reality through which we experience identity and corporeality.

Our breath is nature, our bodies are nature, our spirits are nature. Just as we critique social categories and constructions, we must be critically aware of colonized curriculums and pedagogies that insist that there is no nature-in-learning or learning-in-nature; let us (re)learn there is always both. My turn toward nature writing had been deeply influenced by Robin Wall Kimmerer's *Braiding Sweetgrass: Indigenous Wisdom, Scientific Knowledge, and the Teachings of Plants*[4] and Alexis Pauline Gumbs's *Undrowned: Black Feminist Lessons from Marine Mammals*.[5] Now that my day job centers environmental justice, healthy rivers, and clean water for people and nature, I find my "academic" voice and writing shifting. More and more I am swimming in my creative landscape; nature is now writing me.

Food/Beast

I am also becoming more attentive to foodways, acknowledging the gathering and preparing of the elders has always been medicine. Food is offered up by nature, even if some of the ingredients now have a complicated path to the plate. My father likes to joke that my generation of cousins prefers to eat foods labeled "natural" and "organic." He enjoys pointing out that any food derived of matter, any physical substance, could reasonably be labeled in this way. We laugh, but when we visit the bayou, we still drive the fifty miles into town to the organic market for provisions, an oppressive necessity. The land, water, and people have been poisoned. How do we now harvest? Hansberry notes in the agitation above, "the oppressed are by their nature (i.e., oppressed) forever in ferment." We have oppressed nature. We experience nature's "agitation" against its condition in each famine, flood, drought, storm. Now, we pay for a "better" nature to eat with a whole paycheck.

As a Black queer feminist studies writer, and southern writer, I also grapple with my own attachments to writing nature. My prose, poetry, fiction, and nonfiction are rooted in the land and the nature of Black life, of Black matter that matters. In my narrative portraits and poetry, the Black folk are of the land; some have descriptions or similes from the food and natural world, some are shape-shifters or tricksters who are, themselves, the nature of nature.

White writers have been warned against offensive "food as skin tone" analogies and exoticizing/eroticizing animalistic comparisons, encouraged to decolonize their lens and writing practices. How does a Black queer feminist southern writer reclaim the nature of the body from this critique? How do we as Black and Indigenous People of Color (BIPOC) authors maintain our practices, without sanctioning dehumanizing representations by white writers? How do we root ourselves in the stories of our people and recognize that everything isn't relative as we write our relatives.

Writing ourselves as a part of nature is crucial, our families are delicious recipes, our ancestors are animal apparitions; this is the practice of decolonial writing. Addressing the work of Black gay filmmaker, educator, poet, and activist Marlon Riggs in his chapter "'Quare' Studies, or (Almost) Everything I Know about Queer Studies I Learned from My Grandmother," E. Patrick Johnson writes: "Within this setting [of the woods], Blackness becomes problematically aligned with nature, reinscribing the Black body as bestial and primal."[6]

What if your grandmother appears to family as
A white cat
Suspended raindrops
What if your family's early morning guardian is
An owl
What if the black snake appears every birthday
Cut the head clean off
Use a different knife to cut the cake
What if you hear voices when you eat
Greens
Biscuits
What if she is sugar
A dove
What if he is chocolate

A mule
What if you are
A raven
A ray
Flying

Indeed, Riggs presents us with a primal Black masculinity and sexuality and the material fact of our vulnerable corporeality, sexuality, and morbidity. Johnson continues, "Although Riggs's body signifies in ways that constrain his agency, his embodied blackness also enlivens a discussion of a 'fleshy' nature."[7] My writing lives alongside the tropes that stand critiqued, my body and my stories live in the fleshy nature of my intention.

Homophones

How we sound?

Another question I deeply engage is the sound of the Black south. My apostrophes, abbreviated spellings, and "Black English" or "African American Vernacular English (AAVE)," are inconsistent and chaotic in nature, queer. I grapple with multiple meanings and ways of being, the food and the connection to nature. I also grapple with the nature of speech—both my speech and that of the narrators and speakers I conjure. As griot, how do I reformulate and represent the nature in speech?

I consult the ancestors, as well as context and history from John McWhorter's *Talking Back, Talking Black*[8] and Russell Rickford's *Spoken Soul*,[9] but I seek the nature of dialogue from Hansberry and in the voices of Zora Neale Hurston. The sounds of the living, the dead, and the anthropomorphic earth. The nature of the storm, the nature of nature and what it can do to the body, is captured in the nature of the voice in this passage from *Their Eyes Were Watching God*:

> They made it to a tall house on a hump of ground and Janie said, "Less stop heah. Ah can't make it no further. Ah'm done give out."

"All of us done give out," Tea Cake corrected. "We'se goin'
inside out dis weather, kill or cure."[10]

We know nature killed. You can't run from the weather.

We know Hurston's *Barracoon* came together in 1927 and was
largely unpublished due to its "dialect" (although excerpts were pub-
lished in 2003 by beloved Valerie Boyd[11]) until 2018. As the griot, I
can't run from the nature of the sound of the stories and poems and
praise songs and spells and recipes meant to be read and spoken and
heard—voiced—in my work. Among these are also the elements of
truth. How do I share the nature of my own situatedness?

Academic
Artist
Rural
Urban
Writer
Performer
Conjurer
Lover

The nature of these truth-elements is captured by Frank Marshall
Davis's dark poem, "Arthur Ridgewood, M.D.":

He debated whether
as a poet
to have dreams and beans
or as a physician
have a long car and caviar.
Dividing between both
he died from a nervous breakdown
caused by worry
from rejection slips
and financial notices from the Finance company.[12]

I approach my work, confronting and contending with oppression and violence, gracefully and Black. Existing in the world of the words. The first offering in this section, "Spell for a Bee," celebrates ceremony and the impetus to conjure from a youthful perspective. The second, a poem, in this section, "Thunder Cake," engages the theme of nature and ritual cleansing as lovers creating connection. "Nature Preserve" offers three vignettes, discovering the blurred boundaries between domestic life and the environment, through a child's eyes. "Estuary" is an illustration, inviting the reader into a microcosm of scale. The final entry, "Storm Warning," honors the passing on of ancestral knowledge, about the natural world and our attentiveness, calling us to be present in it.

Nature Invocation for the Reader

May you have
Black joy
   Laugh
   Let
May you have
Meaningful memory
   Mourn
   Make
May you have
Queer longings
   Lust
   Love
May you have
Sonic essentials
   Hear
   Me
   Out
May you have

Culinary yearnings
   Boil
   Down
May you have
Nature
Bayou fête

Spell for a Bee

On the eve of the bee

Find a quiet place
Borrow a pot
Under the back porch
Add termite rot

In a fancy teacup
Fetch bayou mud poo
In a butter dish
Fetch tree sap goo

Fill a thimble
With ant bed sand
Calamine lotion
Slather your hand

Make braids from tiny
Blades of grass
Say your prayers
Like you in mass

Pluck gray curls
From Muh'deah's comb

Shampoo through
Foul gulf seafoam

Break a pen
With dark blue ink
Be sure to do this
Over the sink

Pour the ink
Onto a rose
Wear the petals
Between your toes

From a low oak branch
Untangle moss
Slosh in hot water
And make a sauce

Take a nip
Muscadine wine
Replace with water
Auntie be just fine

Pluck the moths
From the windowsill
Fold them in
A dollar bill

On the morning of the bee

Set out early
Find a frog
Pet its belly
Replace on log

Dress in school clothes
Say a prayer
Wear backwards
Best underwear

Climb under the back porch
With workbook and spell
Speak the words
You'll need to spell

Stir the pot
With magnolia sticks
Check your arms
And legs for ticks

Crumble dry leaves
Add breakfast grits
A thread from the pillow
Where Muh'deah sits

A drop of vinegar
Ignites the spell
Breathe it in
And you'll do well

Recite each word
Spit in the pot
Whisper low
Don't get caught

Now you know your
A B C's
Winner of all
Spelling bees

Passing. Digital photograph by Mel Michelle Lewis, 2023.

Thunder Cake*

In the jar without air holes
Alabama
Bayou stale

Auntie who is kin to me and
Auntie who is kin to you
are preserved like peaches
together
in their own sweetness

raindrops drizzle

Auntie who is kin to me
opens windows
Auntie who is kin to you
turns the dial with one finger until it clicks
to hush the whispering radio

dark clouds seep through their kitchen
moistening the sack of sweet granules
humid sugar clings

* Originally published in *Queer Nature*, ed. Michael Walsh (Philadelphia, PA: Autumn House Press, 2022), 177–178.

Auntie is glistening with Crisco
Auntie is doused in flour

the cake
is cooling

rain comes down in silky gray patches
Auntie who is kin to me and
Auntie who is kin to you
step outside
screen doors swing behind them
smacking doorframes
applauding thunder

red clay becomes smooth between toes
loosening their aprons
they step out of their light summer dresses

fragile faces are lifted to the warmth
droplets roll from dreary rumbling tongues
like sincere compliments

rain saturates their thin slips
flowing over their shoulders

pooling in their clavicles

puddles splash and splatter their calves
with crimson clay
Auntie who is kin to me and
Auntie who is kin to you
return to their kitchen

to put the icing on the Thunder Cake

Nature Preserve

I. REST IN PEACE

"Dis house cold soaked," Papa Heron say. "We done been gone a good while."

I scramble out the back seat of the rust-ate Ford truck.

I carry every backpack, duffel, and plastic bag I can twist around my body or weave through my little hands. I ain't finna come back out once I get up in de house. Mydaddy Beau check all the downstairs rooms. Redbone hound push the doors open with his tangerine nose, sniff every corner, nod yes and smile at Mydaddy Beau with his corn kernel teeth, wag his ham hock body.

Papa Heron light the gas fire, light the wood fire, light the stove fire.

I scramble upstairs with every backpack, duffel, and plastic bag. I know I got to wash up first, but I'm finna get up in de bed and lay up till noon tomorrow. Ain't nuthin like ya own bed.

Redbone hound waddle up behind me, sniff the air, whine like a screen door hinge. He back down on his ham haunches and shake his head no, frown his jowls.

I don't know what done got into him. I roll my eyes, push open my bedroom door with my bloat of bags.

Someone in my bed!

Redbone hound gasp for air and stare. He rise up slow, make his round body into a point with one raised paw. My legs are

molasses, I can't move. My eyes bend the image of a little white
man sleeping serene up in my bed.
His head propped on the pillow, arms outstretched.
Some sounds come from way down in me and Redbone hound.
We howl.

Papa Heron and Mydaddy Beau startle up the staircase cussin. I
can't say dem words. Muh'Deah say ain't no swearing on Gawd in
ya mind, neither. Ain't no repeating after grown folks, not tat'al.
I'm pointing, Redbone hound pointing.
Papa Heron pointing, Mydaddy Beau pointing.
The little white man sleeping serene up in my bed.
"Lawd he must'a come down the chimney," Papa Heron say.
"He splayed out jus'like he sleep," Mydaddy Beau say.

> My eyes unbend
> The little white man got
> A round face
> Pointy toes
> Skinny arms
> Fluffy feathers
> A sharp beak
> Dark talons
> Wide wings

"That theres'de Bayou Barn Owl," Papa Heron say.
Redbone hound nod yes and smile.
Ain't no way I'm finna sleep with him in my bed tonight.

II. SWEET TOOTH
Papa Heron sit at the gas station in the rust-ate Ford truck.
He roll down the window
He smoke cigarettes
He read the newspaper
He drink coffee

He wave at comin and goin
I roll down the window
I suck candy
I look at the funnies
I nap
I shy from comin and goin

On Saturday Saint Catholic Church got a table set up along the
    wall outside the gas station.
They got boxes of doughnuts
They got pictures of starving children
They got a cashbox
They got a Maxwell House tin can for change and dollar bills
They got Saint Catholic Church bulletins
They got Saint Catholic Church prayer pamphlets
They got the ladies of the Sodality of Our Lady

Papa Heron give me $1 for a box of doughnuts.
A box of doughnuts is a $5 donation
The ladies of the Sodality of Our Lady say
You can give Saint Catholic Church a $1 donation
For nothin, or
You can give Saint Church a $5 donation
For something

I splain to Papa Heron what the ladies of the Sodality of Our
    Lady say
He say go ahead and give Saint Church a $1 donation
For nothin
I splain to the ladies of the Sodality of Our Lady what Papa
    Heron say
I give Saint Church a $1 donation
For nothin
I cry like pictures of starving children
The ladies of the Sodality of Our Lady

Have mercy
They give me a box of doughnuts and some blessings
I climb up in the rust-ate Ford truck with my blessed box of
    doughnuts
I splain to Papa Heron we got blessed
I gaze upon the glazed doughnuts through the clear plastic
    church window
I start to pry open the cardboard top
The doughnuts rustle and thwack
The box vibrates in my lap
The doughnuts flutter and scale
Little amber faces emerge
Look back at me through the clear plastic church window
A choir of glazed gorged cockroaches pray

I fling the glazed doughnut box out the window
Of the rust-ate Ford truck
I cry like pictures of starving children

III. ROT
Muh'deah say, cut off the bad
Guh'ment orange cheese don't go bad easy
Dry stale crack
Green lush moss
White ash skin
Cheese is alive
And like ta'killya
But not if you cut the bad off it first

Muh'deah say fish jumpin to see
What we gon fry up for breakfast
Turn your back to the water when you bait that hook
With slimy hot shrimp
Step back behind the oaks
Crouch down behind the truck

Mullet not gon bite the line
If they done seen what you finna do
They gonna tell it
And aint nobody gon bite den
Mullet got a mouth on them

Muh'deah say milk good another day
Smell milk before you pour
Not just the wet sour carton paper
Not just the tart origami wax folds
Armpit and thigh meat whiff
Smell the milk deep down in the well
Milk sour like white folk
Always finna turn
But might be good another day

Muh'deah say wood spoon the best
Split burnt and worn
Baby teething and cousin spanking
Vinegar erosion
Grits ladle
Lost and found
Generation licked
Turn black turn red turn green turn back brown black
Wood spoon a whole tree
Growing out de gumbo

Estuary

Stingray lip smile
Fire ant sculpture
Oak limb tress
Crab fiddle dance
Tidal foam fester
Termite braille script
Croaker dialect eulogy
Magnolia humid fume
Racoon bustle totter
Catfish whisker draggle
Gull laughter riot
Lizard throat pennant
Minnow silver strategy
Pelican stare verdict
Mosquito hunger secret
Shrimp retreat armor
Gator bask pose
Snake question mark
Frog song silence

Lazarus. Digital photograph by Mel Michelle Lewis, 2023.

Storm Warning

Ain't Sallie break the silence of our listening to dusk on the porch. She say, the Ancestors cn'tell a storm coming.

Ain't Sallie tell it, from her weathered white rocking chair, propped up on faded satin pillows like a throne. It was over 'hundred degrees today, and ain't cooled off much yet, but Ain't Sallie pull her knitted cap over her white egret feather head and got the quilt Mama Coosa made when she was just a lil'gal in her lap, down over her little egret legs. The breeze off the gulf barely just high enough to keep the mosquitos from hoverin over, but Ain't Sallie ain't finna catch no chill.

Ain't Sallie say look at the clouds, they tell folks what's commin. They high and mighty and can see all round. They know what's on the way, and sometime bring it they own self. The whole sky try to tell it, if you lookin and listenin. What color is that sky? It got moods just like all beings. Sometime sky wake up mad wit'fire. You got to know how to get ready. Ain't Sallie point her spindly egret finger at the orangepink fading sunset. Sky showin it love us tonight.

Ain't Sallie close her peach cobbler eyes and lift her chin. She say the air'll tell you what you want to know. Is it wet like the breath out your mouth or dry like the breath out your nose? The way the land is breathing say what's commin too. Is the land breathing heavy like runnin or with a light sigh like sleepin? The heavy air get inside your teeth and behind your eyes, make you feel like underwater. Ain't Sallie say ask the old folks how they es. She rub her egret knees and run her hand up and down her thigh over the quilt. Old folk can tell from they insides when things are a'changin. Heavy air get in the folding parts of the body, make us move slow.

Ain't Sallie clap her hands softly and open her eyes. She say the birds can tell it to you. Sometimes they show you by how they roost in a tree, fly low, or sometimes they change their song, tellin each other how it's finna be. Other times they all disappear and the air is empty. Sometimes a bird somebody who ain't supposed to be around come around; he always got a story to tell if you sit and listen. Ain't Sallie laugh out loud. She light up her pipe again and lean back and rock a while. She say bird ain't never lost, he just ain't where he sposedto be sometime, like menfolk. She scrunch up her face and chuckle inside her soft downy feather chest. She let out a smile of smoke.

Ain't Sallie rock in her chair a while, then say dembugs know what bout to happen too. Listen for they song, old folks know all the meanings. Some of em mean good weather come gimme some sugar, other sounds mean it ain't the right time on account of the weather. Silent mean erybody gone, they done dug underground or flew off. When the ants work double time and the ant-hills get tall, just you wait for a storm.

Ain't Sallie adjust herself on her throne, she pat her pillows and double her quilt over in her lap. She say the fish and all the ocean somebodies got to tell it too. Ain't nobody hungry for the hook or the trap when the big storm commin in. Ain't no crabs or fish or rays or nobody wet near the shore for days. Ain't nuthin in the net. Everybody wet got to go way down in the deep water where it quiet and just set.

Ain't Sallie take a deep breath and open her eyes wide like a cat. She make her palms like she prayin. Ancestors cn'tell the living bout the weather if we just set still and listen. Memba'when it was on your heart to take in the laundry off the line on a bright sunny afternoon, and de rain storm come up on you just as you finish? Memba'when you sprung a little leak in de'boat and spent half the day pluggin it then was out of gas before you was even out the bayou and de lightning came a'crashin and the water spout rose up just where you was bout to be fishin? Memba'when you was finna hitch the mule to the carriage and they wouldn't budge then you was finna knock his eyes out and give'em a whuppin but he bit ya backside? Just as you came in fa'me to patch you up the storm came and flooded the road and washed out the bridge you woulda been on? Memba when you wasn't finna have no baby that day but baby done'came, and you got carried up to ya sista house in town and the hurricane came and washed through the house you woulda been up in it? She light up her pipe again and lean back and rock a while. Memba?

Ain't Sallie break the silence of our listening to night on the porch. She say, the Ancestors cn'tell a storm coming.

Rue Brew. Digital photograph by Mel Michelle Lewis, 2023.

Return Portal

Last night I dreamed of ceremony.

The medicine people and diviners sanctified the space. They unfurled fabrics, they tied scarves, they conjured themselves into non-human Divine.

Healer Woman came and covered me, bending me in her billowing dress and shawl. She pulled her clasped fist, into the place where sharp ribs open soft. I heaved, and pleaded, "I'm not choking."

I am fluent in a known language I have never heard awake, but always feel the sound and remember. I rouse with translations.

"Not choking, not choking." She affirmed that I was.

She pulled and thrusted. I pleaded and lurched. I felt phlegm building in my throat. Asphyxiant forming. I spit out an orb of burgundy gelatin.

Healer Woman said, "the perfect that does not exist," in the known language and pointed her charcoal slurry finger.

The ceremony continued. Healer Woman put a bowl on my head.

Upsidedown.

Empty bowl, full of heavy. My neck sprang, I fidgeted, it fell, I caught it in my hands.

Rightsideup.

I drowned, in waves of disappointment. "Not right, not right."

Healer Woman said, "the perfect that does not exist," and pointed her fruit inked finger.

Last night I dreamed of dancing.

The French Quarter performers took turns, a New Orleans jazz and tap audition. Dressed in young Black cool and moving in fluid syncopated motion, they danced.

My feet were slew-foot slow. My motions were lard and lemons.

The musician paused and said to me, "Jazz is the music of the heart."

"Tap is the rhythm of the body," I replied.

"Blues is the song of the soul," the singer said.

I danced the old body and bones dance.

I was a heel dig history.

Adams/Lewis

Yesterday they opened the Africatown Heritage House. My family attended. There was a wreath, there was a Ju'ly heat index, there was a reading of the names, there was water. Adams, Lewis, our names read aloud in hot hazy who and how order. Who your people? Here we are. We are "the perfect that does not exist."

> I write this to say
> Who I am
> To say
> What I know
> To say
> Unknown made
> Still
> Can not be unmade

As a child I learned to recite the Nicene Creed. I continued ascending. I am the ancestors ". . . of heaven and earth, of all that is seen and unseen." We are "begotten not made." A prayer. A history.

Invitation

We designed an invitation.
To send the masses.
.jpeg .pdf text message email send the rsvp
Out
4 P.M.
Saturday
August
Down to the house.
For my parents.
And for Kerrie.
And for me.
To go, *down to the house.*
There is a plan.

My wife and I will arrive in a few weeks, for the party. Not our party, but my parents' yearly bayou fête. Birthday and years, marriage and years, storm and years, years and years. The Menu has been finalized. They got fried shrimp, catfish, chicken tenders, roast chicken, baked beans, coleslaw, potato salad, rolls, hush puppies, sweet tea, cake, and Blue Bell Homemade Vanilla ice cream. We are invited.

Although I have lived far away for many tides, I am in my season of return. I've never felt closer and more of this land and water and people. I've needed to say all that has been said, to untangle the fishing line, to patch the leaky hull, to chart a course back home. Repair requires art. Restoration requires retelling the biomythic self. My roots are reaching for home.

Biomythography Bayou is a ritual.

Portal Invocation for the Author

By now
There have been hurricanes

Burials
Births
Ise getting to be

Bout time
To go
Down to the house

By now
Your car has broken down
Your back has gone out
Your arthritis has flared
Your eyes have blurred
Your hip has refused
(the car has been fixed)

By now
We have gotten vaccinated
A lot
We have gotten sick
We have gotten well
A lot

By now
You are happier
You are slower
You are rounder
You are deeper
You are auntie
You are griot
You are seer
You are artist
(I am)

Just now
They've found a prehistoric

Gulf Sturgeon
Floating
Down to the house
White armor
Griot
Keeper of ancient time
Emerged from the depths
To call
You home

We are going.

Notes

Conjure Portal

1. Malidoma Patrice Somé, *The Healing Wisdom of Africa: Finding Life Purpose through Nature* (New York: Tarcher, 1999); Malidoma Patrice Somé, *Of Water and the Spirit: Ritual, Magic, and Initiation in the Life of an African Shaman* (New York: Putnam, 1994); and Malidoma Patrice Somé, "Elemental Rituals," https://malidoma.com/main/elemental -rituals/.

2. Stacey Floyd-Thomas and Laura Gillman, "'The Whole Story Is What I'm After'": Womanist Revolutions and Liberation Feminist Revelations through Biomythography and Emancipatory Historiography," *Black Theology* 3, no. 2 (2005): 184.

3. Andrea C. Walker and David E. Balk, "Bereavement Rituals in the Muscogee Creek Tribe," *Death Studies* 31, no. 7 (2007): 635–636.

Part 1 Water

1. Zora Neale Hurston, *Barracoon: The Story of the Last "Black Cargo,"* ed. Deborah G. Plant, 1st ed. (New York: Amistad, 2018), 24.

2. Hurston, *Barracoon*, 24.

3. Hurston, *Barracoon*, 72.

4. Hurston, *Barracoon*, 3.

5. M. Jacqui Alexander, *Pedagogies of Crossing: Meditations on Feminism, Sexual Politics, Memory, and the Sacred* (Durham, NC: Duke University Press, 2006), 162.

6. Tiffany Lethabo King, *The Black Shoals: Offshore Formations of Black and Native Studies* (Durham, NC: Duke University Press, 2019), 31.

7. Edna Lewis, *The Taste of Country Cooking* (New York: Knopf, 2012), xxi.

8. Vanessa Knights and Ian D. Biddle, *Music, National Identity, and the Politics of Location: Between the Global and the Local* (New York: Routledge, 2007), 42.

9. Kim TallBear, "Why Interspecies Thinking Needs Indigenous Standpoints," *Fieldsights*, November 18, 2011.

Part 2   Fire

1. Octavia E. Butler, *Parable of the Sower* (New York: Grand Central Publishing, 2000).

2. Evie Shockley, *semiautomatic* (Middletown, CT: Wesleyan University Press, 2017), 9.

3. Tanisha C. Ford, *Liberated Threads: Black Women, Style, and the Global Politics of Soul* (Chapel Hill: University of North Carolina Press, 2015), 5.

4. Janell Hobson, *Body as Evidence: Mediating Race, Globalizing Gender* (Albany: SUNY Press, 2012), 67.

5. Britney Cooper, *Eloquent Rage: A Black Feminist Discovers Her Superpower* (New York: St. Martin's, 2018), 275.

Part 3   Earth

1. Alice Walker, *In Search of Our Mothers' Gardens: Womanist Prose* (New York: Houghton Mifflin Harcourt, 2004), 17.

2. Walker, *In Search of Our Mothers' Gardens*, 17, 21.

3. Walker, *In Search of Our Mothers' Gardens*, 21.

4. Jessye Norman, "Dido and Aeneas, Z. 626: Thy hand, Belinda . . . When I am laid in earth," on *The Essential Jessye Norman*, recorded 2000, Baarn, Netherlands, Philips, compact disc.

5. James Baldwin, *Giovanni's Room* (London: Everyman's Library, 2016), 158.

6. "Poarch Creek Indian Tribe: Tribal Enrollment," on the website of the Poarch Creek Indians, accessed January 20, 2021, https://pci-nsn.gov/tribal-enrollment/.

Part 4   Mineral

1. Toni Cade Bambara, *The Salt Eaters* (New York: Vintage, 1992), 7.
2. Maya Angelou, "On the Pulse of Morning," in *The Complete Collected Poems of Maya Angelou* (New York: Random House, 1994), 269–273.
3. Tera W. Hunter, *Bound in Wedlock: Slave and Free Black Marriage in the Nineteenth Century* (Cambridge, MA: Harvard University Press, 2017), 6.
4. Catherine E. McKinley, *Afrekete: An Anthology of Black Lesbian Writing* (New York: Anchor, 1995), xii.
5. Audre Lorde, *Zami: A New Spelling of My Name: A Biomythography* (Toronto: Crossing Press, 2011), 255.
6. Audre Lorde, "Sisters in Arms," in *The Collected Poems of Audre Lorde* (New York: W. W. Norton & Company, 2000), 255–357.
7. David Alsobrook, "Fallen Doves," *Mobile Bay Magazine*, February 2014, https://mobilebaymag.com/fallen-doves/.
8. Richard Wright, "Red Clay Blues," in *Richard Wright Reader*, vol. 774 (Cambridge, MA: Da Capo Press, 1997), 247.
9. Michael Twitty, *The Cooking Gene: A Journey through African American Culinary History in the Old South* (New York: Amistad, 2018).
10. Gwendolyn Brooks, "An Aspect of Love, Alive in the Ice and Fire," in *Riot* (Detroit, MI: Broadside Press, 1969), 21–22.

Part 5   Nature

1. Lorraine Hansberry, "Simone de Beauvoir and *The Second Sex*: An American Commentary," in *Words of Fire: An Anthology of African-American Feminist Thought*, edited by Beverly Guy-Sheftall (New York: The New Press, 1995), 128–142.
2. Malidoma Patrice Somé, *Of Water and the Spirit: Ritual, Magic, and Initiation in the Life of an African Shaman* (New York: Putnam, 1994), 262–263.

3. Alice Walker, *In Search of Our Mothers' Gardens: Womanist Prose* (New York: Houghton Mifflin Harcourt, 2004), xii.

4. Robin Wall Kimmerer, *Braiding Sweetgrass: Indigenous Wisdom, Scientific Knowledge, and the Teachings of Plants* (Minneapolis, MN: Milkweed Editions, 2013).

5. Alexis Pauline Gumbs, *Undrowned: Black Feminist Lessons from Marine Mammals* (Chico, CA: AK Press, 2001).

6. E. Patrick Johnson, "'Quare' Studies, or (Almost) Everything I Know about Queer Studies I Learned from My Grandmother," *Text and Performance Quarterly* 21, no. 1 (2001): 1–25.

7. Johnson, "'Quare' Studies," 1–25.

8. John McWhorter, *Talking Back, Talking Black: Truths about America's Lingua Franca* (New York: Bellevue Literary Press, 2016).

9. Russell John Rickford, *Spoken Soul: The Story of Black English* (New York: John Wiley & Sons Incorporated, 2000).

10. Zora Neale Hurston, *Their Eyes Were Watching God* (New York: Harper Collins, 1998), 162.

11. Valerie Boyd, *Wrapped in Rainbows: The Life of Zora Neale Hurston* (New York: Simon and Schuster, 2003).

12. Frank Marshall Davis, "Aurthur Ridgewood, M.D.," in *The Black Poets*, ed. Dudley Randall (New York: Bantam, 1988), 121.

Bibliography

Alexander, M. Jacqui. *Pedagogies of Crossing: Meditations on Feminism, Sexual Politics, Memory, and the Sacred*. Durham, NC: Duke University Press, 2006, 162.

Allison, Dorothy. *Bastard out of Carolina: A Novel*. New York: Penguin, 2005.

———. *Skin: Talking about Sex, Class, and Literature*. New York: Open Road Media Firebrand Books, 2005.

Angelou, Maya. "On the Pulse of Morning." In *The Complete Collected Poems of Maya Angelou*. New York: Random House, 1994, 269–273.

Baldwin, James. *Giovanni's Room*. London: Everyman's Library, 2016, 158.

Bambara, Toni Cade. *The Salt Eaters*. New York: Vintage, 1992, 7.

Brooks, Gwendolyn. "An Aspect of Love, Alive in the Ice and Fire." In *Riot*. Detroit, MI: Broadside Press, 1969, 21–22.

———. *We Real Cool*. Detroit, MI: Broadside Press, 1959.

Brooks, Gwendolyn, and Elizabeth Alexander. *The Essential Gwendolyn Brooks*. New York: Library of America, 2005.

brown, adrienne m. *Pleasure Activism: The Politics of Feeling Good*. Chico, CA: AK Press, 2019.

Butler, Octavia E. *Parable of the Sower*. New York: Grand Central Publishing, 2000.

Cooper, Britney. *Eloquent Rage: A Black Feminist Discovers Her Superpower*. New York: St. Martin's, 2018.

Cressler, Matthew J. "Black Catholic Conversion and the Burden of Black Religion." *Journal of Africana Religion* 2, no. 2 (2014): 280–287.

Davis, Frank Marshall. "Aurthur Ridgewood, M.D." In *The Black Poets*, edited by Dudley Randall, 121. New York: Bantam, 1988.

De Veaux, Alexis. *Yabo*. New Orleans, LA: Redbone Press, 2014.

Douny, Laurence. *Living in a Landscape of Scarcity: Materiality and Cosmology in West Africa*. Vol. 63. Walnut Creek, CA: Left Coast Press, 2014.

Fayard, Kelly N. "'We've Always Known Who We Are': Belonging in the Poarch Band of Creek Indians." PhD diss., University of Michigan, 2011.

Feinberg, Leslie. *Stone Butch Blues*. New York: Alyson Books, 2004.

Feinstein, Sascha, and Yusef Komunyakaa, eds. *The Jazz Poetry Anthology*. Vol. 637. Bloomington: Indiana University Press, 1991.

Floyd-Thomas, Stacey, and Laura Gillman. "'The Whole Story Is What I'm After': Womanist Revolutions and Liberation Feminist Revelations through Biomythography and Emancipatory Historiography." *Black Theology* 3, no. 2 (2005): 176–199.

Ford, Tanisha C. *Liberated Threads: Black Women, Style, and the Global Politics of Soul*. Chapel Hill: University of North Carolina Press, 2015, 5.

Franklin, Sara B., ed. *Edna Lewis: At the Table with an American Original*. Chapel Hill: University of North Carolina Press, 2018, 106.

Griffin, Susan. *The Eros of Everyday Life: Essays on Ecology, Gender and Society*. New York: Anchor, 1996.

Gumbs, Alexis Pauline. *M Archive: After the End of the World*. Durham, NC: Duke University Press, 2018.

———. *Undrowned: Black Feminist Lessons from Marine Mammals*. Chico, CA: AK Press, 2001.

Hansberry, Lorraine. "Simone de Beauvoir and *The Second Sex*: An American Commentary." In *Words of Fire: An Anthology of African-American Feminist Thought*, edited by Beverly Guy-Sheftall, 128–142. New York: The New Press, 1995.

Hobson, Janell. *Body as Evidence: Mediating Race, Globalizing Gender*. Albany: SUNY Press, 2012, 67.

Hunter, Tera W. *Bound in Wedlock: Slave and Free Black Marriage in the Nineteenth Century*. Cambridge, MA: Harvard University Press, 2017, 6.

Hurston, Zora Neale. *Barracoon: The Story of the Last "Black Cargo."* Edited by Deborah G. Plant. 1st ed. New York: Amistad, 2018.

————. *Their Eyes Were Watching God*. New York: Harper Collins, 1998.

Johnson, E. Patrick. "'Quare' Studies, or (Almost) Everything I Know about Queer Studies I Learned from My Grandmother." *Text and Performance Quarterly* 21, no. 1 (2001): 1–25.

Judd, Bettina. *Patient: Poems*. New York: Black Lawrence Press, 2014.

Kimmerer, Robin. *Braiding Sweetgrass: Indigenous Wisdom, Scientific Knowledge, and the Teachings of Plants*. Minneapolis, MN: Milkweed Editions, 2013.

King, Tiffany Lethabo. *The Black Shoals: Offshore Formations of Black and Native Studies*. Durham, NC: Duke University Press, 2019, 31.

Knights, Vanessa, and Ian D. Biddle. *Music, National Identity, and the Politics of Location: Between the Global and the Local*. New York: Routledge, 2007, 42.

Lewis, Edna. *The Taste of Country Cooking*. New York: Knopf, 2012, xxi.

Lewis, M. "Catfish Mardi Gras Queen." *Auburn Avenue*, Autumn/Winter 2019. https://www.theauburnavenue.com/the-gender-issue.

————. "Thunder Cake." In *Queer Nature*, edited by Michael Walsh, 177–178. Philadelphia, PA: Autumn House Press, 2022.

Lorde, Audre. "Sisters in Arms." In *The Collected Poems of Audre Lorde*. New York: W. W. Norton & Company, 2000, 255–257.

————. *Zami: A New Spelling of My Name: A Biomythography*. Toronto, ON: Crossing Press, 2011.

McKinley, Catherine E. *Afrekete: An Anthology of Black Lesbian Writing*. New York: Anchor, 1995, xii.

McWhorter, John. *Talking Back, Talking Black: Truths about America's Lingua Franca*. New York: Bellevue Literary Press, 2016.

Norman, Jessye. "Dido and Aeneas, Z. 626: Thy hand, Belinda . . . When I am laid in earth." On *The Essential Jessye Norman*. Recorded 2000. Baarn, Netherlands. Philips, compact disc.

Perdue, Theda. "The Legacy of Indian Removal." *Journal of Southern History* 78, no. 1 (2012): 3–36.

"Poarch Creek Indian Tribe: Tribal Enrollment." On the website of the Poarch Creek Indians. Accessed January 20, 2023. https://pci-nsn.gov/tribal-enrollment/.

Ras, Michael Brown, Joan C. Bristol, Emily Suzanne Clark, Michael
Pasquier, Matthew J. Cressler, and Stephen Selka. "Black Catholi-
cism." *Journal of Africana Religions* 2, no. 2 (2014): 244–295.

Rickford, Russell John. *Spoken Soul: The Story of Black English.* New York:
John Wiley & Sons Incorporated, 2000.

Shockley, Evie. *semiautomatic.* Middletown, CT: Wesleyan University
Press, 2017, 9.

Somé, Malidoma Patrice. *The Healing Wisdom of Africa: Finding Life
Purpose through Nature.* New York: Tarcher, 1999.

———. *Of Water and the Spirit: Ritual, Magic, and Initiation in the Life of
an African Shaman.* New York: Putnam, 1994.

TallBear, Kim. "Why Interspecies Thinking Needs Indigenous Stand-
points." *Fieldsights,* November 18, 2011.

Teish, Luisah. *Jambalaya: The Natural Woman's Book of Personal Charms and
Practical Rituals.* New York: Harper & Row, 1985.

Twitty, Michael. *The Cooking Gene: A Journey through African American
Culinary History in the Old South.* 1st ed. New York: Amistad, 2018.

Walker, Alice. *In Search of Our Mothers' Gardens: Womanist Prose.* New
York: Houghton Mifflin Harcourt, 2004, 17, 21.

Walker, Andrea C., and David E. Balk. "Bereavement Rituals in the
Muscogee Creek Tribe." *Death Studies* 31, no. 7 (2007): 633–652.

Willis, George Paul. "Representation, Public Practices, and Women of the
Poarch Band of Creek Indians." PhD diss., University of Alabama,
2020.

Wright, Richard. "Red Clay Blues." In *Richard Wright Reader,* vol. 774.
Cambridge, MA: Da Capo Press, 1997, 247.

Index

About the Author

MEL MICHELLE LEWIS (she/they) is vice president for people, justice, and cultural affairs at American Rivers, providing strategic guidance on social and environmental justice initiatives and creative visioning for the future of clean water and healthy rivers. Dr. Mel is also a collaborator with the Art of Change Agency and an affiliated researcher with the Penn Program in Environmental Humanities at the University of Pennsylvania. Prior to joining American Rivers, Dr. Mel was associate professor and director of the Ecosystems, Sustainability, and Justice Program, cofounder of the Space for Creative Black Imagination: An Interdisciplinary Making and Research Institute, and chair of the Humanistic Studies Department at Maryland Institute College of Art. Previously, they also chaired the Center for Geographies of Justice, the Women, Gender, and Sexuality Studies Department, and the Africana Studies Department at Goucher College, as well as the Department of Ethnic Studies at Saint Mary's College of California. Rooted in the Gulf South's nature, folklore, dialect, foodways, music, and art, their creative work explores queer of color nature writing themes in rural coastal settings. Dr. Mel currently resides in Baltimore. Read more about them at melmichellelewis.com.